BREAKING THROUGH CONCRETE

BREAKING THROUGH CONCRETE
BUILDING AN URBAN FARM REVIVAL

DAVID HANSON AND **EDWIN MARTY**

PHOTOGRAPHS BY MICHAEL HANSON
FOREWORD BY MARK WINNE

UNIVERSITY OF CALIFORNIA PRESS   Berkeley   Los Angeles   London

CONTENTS

FOREWORD
MARK WINNE

As a kid growing up in northern New Jersey, I acutely felt the tension between urban development and the fleeting remnants of a pastoral landscape. Living at the retreating edge of the Garden State's former agrarian glory, I often wondered how Mother Earth could survive the onslaught of macadam, concrete, plastic, steel, and rubber. I would eventually find a kind of perverse solace in the hearty blades of grass and indefatigable dandelion shoots that muscled their way through the fissures in roadways and parking lots. They told me better than any science textbook could that no matter what abuse humankind may heap on our planet, nature will not only survive but one day triumph.

Yet we don't need to wait (or, in bleaker moments, hope) for some kind of Armageddon to wash away our mess. The satisfying and edifying stories told in *Breaking Through Concrete* make it abundantly clear that humanity's need to allow nature to flourish may matter even more than nature's will to survive. Urban farming, gardening, and growing—or whatever you want to call the phenomenon that is altering the definition of conventional food production—is catching on faster than veggie wraps. Turning over manicured sod at 1600 Pennsylvania Avenue, removing rubble and covering old parking lots with compost in Rust Belt Detroit, and raising growing beds on Brooklyn rooftops the way a community used to raise barns are the stories of the day.

Skeptics, of course, abound. Spokespersons for Big Farming and Big Food have turned their noses up at these so-called urban aesthetes and utopian farmers whose acreage is so small that it can barely support a rototiller. But with a billion of the globe's people hungry, a second billion undernourished, and another billion obese, conventional and industrial forms of agriculture have hardly earned bragging rights.

The Homeless Garden Project in Santa Cruz, California, like all the urban farms we encountered, has a bustling energy that both stems from and adds to the urban world around it.

Urban food production may not feed a hungry world, but as *Breaking Through Concrete* amply demonstrates, it can feed a hungry spirit and a hunger for both nature and human connection. And as the world becomes less food secure every day, growing food in unconventional places will be thought of no longer as a nicety, like a flower box of petunias slung from a brownstone's windowsill, but as a necessity born out of the looming realization that there will be nine billion of us to feed by 2050. At the very least, urban farming can be thought of as an insurance policy with a modest monthly premium, or as a hedge fund with no downside risk.

As a child of the sixties, my worldview was shaped as much by the devastation of the moment as it was by a wild, fantastical notion of the future. While Joni Mitchell may have told us, "They paved paradise and put up a parking lot," *Breaking Through Concrete* reminds us that we can also rip up the parking lot and liberate paradise.

Edwin Marty and I started talking about a book on urban farms at the Garage Café in the Southside neighborhood of Birmingham, Alabama. It is one of those eccentric dives that seem to populate the South more than any other region. The back courtyard is shaded by old trees that force their way out of the uneven patio and stretch their twisted branches over the chunky concrete tables and wobbly benches. Rooms filled with teetering stacks of wrought-iron antiques and statuary only sometimes for sale are closed off by sliding glass doors that look into the courtyard.

It's the kind of place where ideas hatch. I've known Edwin for years because we both worked for the same magazine-publishing group in town. Edwin eventually went full-time into Jones Valley Urban Farm and urban agriculture consulting, and I began to follow smart-growth developments with the magazine I worked for at the time. We both saw the trends happening: new farmer visionaries planting their ideas in neighborhoods and towns around the country, and an emerging market of consumers seeking a connection to their food. And the scenes and the stories and the people were inspiring.

But we didn't see any publications that celebrated the new American urban farm movement. The buzz around urban farms is flourishing, as expected considering the increase in farmer's markets, the trend of farm-to-plate restaurants, and the food-focused media in many cities. But many farms and food-garden projects around the country still exist in their own little bubbles, and the large percentage of Americans who have recently come to appreciate the idea of "organic" seem unaware of not only the presence of urban farms in most American cities but also the discussion within the farm movement of what an urban farm *is*. And the urban farm is many things.

So, back in the Garage, we decided we should collect the stories and images from a representative selection of American urban farms as they exist in 2010. We searched the country for the best examples of the diverse ways urban farms operate and benefit their communities. We put it all down in a big book proposal and the University of California Press bit.

Uh-oh. Now we actually had to make this happen. This was January 2010. On May 19, 2010, my brother, photographer Michael Hanson; videographer and friend Charlie Hoxie; and I left Seattle, Washington, in a short Blue Bird school bus named Lewis Lewis. The remodeled interior slept three and had a kitchen and two work desks. The engine ran on diesel and recycled vegetable oil. We had two months and over a dozen cities to visit between Seattle, New Orleans, Brooklyn, and Chicago.

The journey took us into a rich vein of American entrepreneurialism. The old spirit of opportunity and optimism was bursting at the seams in the farms we encountered. Each stop along our counterclockwise cross-country ramble inspired us with new ideas and different faces speaking eloquently and passionately about helping their communities.

There might not be a better way to see America right now than via a short bus smoking fry grease. We connected with urban farmers, of course. But we also spent (too much) time with diesel mechanics, with cops in small-town Arkansas, and with biodiesel greasers selling or giving away their salvaged "fuel." In Vona, Colorado, while eating dinner beside Lewis Lewis and watching the setting sun light up a grain silo, we met the families of large-scale agriculture. More than once, we were roused from sleep in the middle of the night and kicked out of mall parking lots. A school bus spray painted white and traveling at 55 miles per hour sparks the curiosity of many of the people it passes, and that's mostly a good thing.

Unfortunately, Lewis Lewis refused to budge from Birmingham's Jones Valley Urban Farm, which was appropriate. You see, the bus was named after Edwin's first employee, Lewis Nelson Lewis, a homeless man in Birmingham who began helping Edwin at the Southside garden. He worked hard, if sporadically, and Edwin eventually hired him. Lewis became a staple of any farm activity, and it's not a stretch to say that Edwin and the farm were his lifeblood. Lewis Lewis passed away on April 20, 2009. It's no wonder Lewis Lewis the Bus did not want to leave his farm. We continued on our route up the East Coast in a white minivan, though we undoubtedly lost a spirit of adventure.

Breaking Through Concrete is a result of that road trip and a decade of urban farming experience. We share the stories of twelve farms, and we give the inside scoop on the dos and don'ts of urban farming. While the Garage Café fostered our early conversations, the urban farms sprouting around America are serving as the think tanks for the food revolution that must and, thankfully, is happening in our country. Hopefully, what we've found developing in America's cities on a small scale can spread into the prime farmland and the larger economy and germinate a sustainable solution to our current food and nutrition problems. Not many things say hope like green leaves breaking through concrete.

Walking the streets of Birmingham's Southside neighborhood, I step carefully along the cracked sidewalks and hop through the kudzu creeping across vacant lots. Kudzu, brought to America from Asia to feed livestock, is now an invasive part of every overgrown landscape in the South. My eyes follow the vine's homogenizing green layer of vegetation as it actively engulfs trees and abandoned buildings. By the time I walk back this way later in the afternoon, another tree and more breaks in the sidewalk will be covered, or so it seems on this hot late-summer day. I know Birmingham is not that different from most other cities across America. Get off the beaten path and you'll find the urban infrastructure falling apart, with invasive weeds breaking through the concrete. Too often it reflects the unraveling of a community's fabric, as well.

I also know that kudzu can't be blamed for distorting the lifeless lines of a city block. It is just doing what it does best: filling in the voids. In its native setting, kudzu covers up soil exposed by natural disasters, such as earthquakes and fires. From an ecological perspective, cities present a similar form: acres of exposed soil and disrupted natural landscapes. Kudzu doesn't notice the difference. So the battle lines are drawn and homeowners and landscape crews work tirelessly to keep the kudzus of the world at bay, proving the supremacy of man by maintaining monocropped landscapes of grass and concrete.

There is, of course, deep irony in the spread of kudzu across Birmingham. Long ago, the city outlawed the livestock that would happily be eating the nutritious green kudzu leaves. Even though the politicians' intentions—keeping the public safe by protecting the municipal water from the dangers of manure—were perhaps noble, this

An intern plows a field at the Homeless Garden Project. Her youth and passion epitomize what drives the urban farm revival in America.

legal separation of the city from its food system put into action steps that inevitably created a broken system. Birmingham is now just like most municipalities in America, a city devoid of access to fresh, healthy food, a problem that contributes directly to skyrocketing rates of obesity and other diet-related issues.

Etching Out an Urban Farm

In the fall of 2001, I clearly saw the battle against kudzu being lost along Tenth Avenue South. But instead of lamenting the green tide of overgrowth, I felt a surge of inspiration. I'd moved back to my home to embrace the urban decay as an indicator of opportunity. Wherever there is broken concrete, there is a chance for life to appear. Employ an adequate dose of intention, and that life can support healthy human communities. With thoughts of urban revival firmly embedded in my head, I helped start Jones Valley Urban Farm that same autumn. My partner, Page Allison, and I carved out a portion of a kudzu-covered hillside and started growing food for local upscale farmer's markets and restaurants.

A contrarian view of urban decay had its roots in my childhood, in the newly emerging suburbs of Birmingham. My family's home was built on concrete freshly poured over thick Alabama woodlands. We had moved to one of the first "true" suburbs constructed in the Birmingham area. By "true" suburb, I mean homes built with no connection to a city center and with no particular thought put into the suburb's planning. These were houses constructed for people interested in living away from the turbulent, racially charged inner city. I can't fault my parents; they raised our family in a safe community with good schools. But they did lay the foundation for my interest in urban restoration. In the mid-1980s, I would head downtown with high-school friends to explore the empty streets and buildings of Birmingham. Nothing was happening in the city. Thousands of acres were home to quietly rusting steel mills, vacated towering bank buildings, and railroads lined with graffiti-covered brick warehouses. It baffled me. Why was no one investing in the city? The answer is long and convoluted.

My response was simple: leave. And so after high school, most of my friends and I scattered across the country. I found myself at the University of Oregon, exploring the radically different ways Eugene city planners confronted urban issues. When I arrived, Eugene had just closed the city center to automobile traffic. Traffic circles were everywhere, slowing the flow of automobiles. Community gardens outnumbered vacant lots. For a kid from the suburbs of Birmingham, it was mesmerizing. Back home, we didn't even have sidewalks, or anyone interested in talking about them.

As part of Eugene's progressive urban planning, the university offered a class called Urban Farming, taught by an architecture professor named Richard Britz. He spent the first semester telling his captive audience of dreamy, wide-eyed students how cities in other countries were decades ahead of the United States in developing sustainable models for their urban landscape. He offered examples from every part of the world where local, sustainable food systems were blossoming through the cracking concrete. The second semester we helped break ground for the urban farm on campus. The wheels were spinning in my head. For the first time in my life I was seeing a productive way to address the decay that plagued Birmingham. Professor Britz was pointing a way to turn the liabilities in cities into assets.

After college, I followed in some of the footsteps of my professor. I visited progressive models of urban farms in Vancouver, Canada; Melbourne, Australia; and Beijing, China. The seed that had been planted kept growing. When I would visit my parents for the holidays in Birmingham, I would drive through the still-empty streets wondering why no one was capitalizing on all the opportunity I saw.

But it wasn't until Page and I finished up a season of managing an organic farm in Baja that our vision took hold. We both thought it would be a great time to move back to Alabama to farm where the market for locally grown organic produce was surprisingly strong, with new farmer's markets popping up and high-end restaurants unable to find quality products. We briefly discussed starting a traditional rural farm in Alabama's Black Belt, but we were concerned about the social isolation. An urban farm seemed the perfect fit. So on the morning of September 11, 2001, we packed up our truck and spent the next three days driving across a nation stunned by the terrorist events in New York and Washington, D.C. The somber mood of the country, as told by the passing NPR stations we were glued to, bolstered our conviction that we were on the right path.

We arrived in Birmingham and found a city deeply affected by the acts of 9/11. Fear and distrust were at an all-time high, and that's saying something in a city known for church bombings and fire hoses. Had I had more experience in nonprofits, I might have also realized that the climate for funding new projects, ones that weren't focused on "homeland security," was at an all-time low. But Page and I persevered. We solicited everyone we knew for vacant land and eventually ended up finding a small, abandoned lot covered in kudzu. We dug in.

Although in time Page moved on to other growing opportunities, I've spent the last ten years developing Jones Valley Urban Farm into a thriving nonprofit, with over twenty-eight acres that produce healthy food and provide educational programs to thousands of youths and adults throughout the city. The farm's vision has evolved from focusing primarily on transforming vacant lots into productive farms to contributing to the slow but steady progression toward a more sustainable food system, a return to a consciousness about health and food and community.

Abundant Urban Models

Not surprisingly, I've found that the things that motivated me to commit my life to farming in the city were not unique. A dedicated core of urban farm entrepreneurs has emerged among my generation that sits somewhere between the hippies of the 1960s and Generation Y. Jones Valley Urban Farm is just one of the hundreds of projects started in the last decade that are responding to the opportunities in modern American cities. While good urban planning promotes dense land use, it is rarely achieved, and over time a waning of intensity inevitably sets in. It is nearly impossible for planners to create a contingency plan for what will happen if a strip mall fails, a new interstate project cuts off a community, or a housing development isn't fully occupied. In the past, kudzu in the South, blackberries in Seattle, or garlic mustard in Detroit filled this void.

But early in this century, farmers across the United States radically shifted the battle lines of urban development and urban decay. No longer are invasive species given a decade's head start. Coupled with a significant resurgence of interest in local food, farmers are staking claim to open urban space and finding fertile ground beneath the canopy of neglect. Although urban farming is far from a new endeavor (the Persians were composting urban waste in 1000 B.C.E.), a significant boom in interest has occurred around the country in the last decade, and it has a broad and varied community. Unlike previous waves of interest in urban farming, the blossoming of projects in the twenty-first century cuts cleanly across racial and demographic profiles. Cities such as Detroit have been experimenting with urban farm projects for well over a hundred years. But the previous attempts were usually government-funded endeavors intended to "dig" out of a recession or provide stimulus to the local economy through job creation.

The latest wave of urban farming is harder to classify. Community gardens with roots dating back decades are still thriving in cities like New York and Seattle. School gardens are being linked with hands-on science classes and changing what's served in the cafeterias. For-profit farms are taking advantage of a trend toward purchasing locally produced food at farmer's markets. And still more nonprofit urban farms are providing job training and social services.

Breaking Through Concrete documents the new wave of urban farming in America and puts a name on the faces working out in the fields surrounded by buildings. Who are these people changing the look of urban communities and what are their motives? Are they acting in isolation or are they part of a larger shift in consciousness throughout the country?

What Is an Urban Farm?

During talks and lectures about Jones Valley Urban Farm, I find myself regularly answering the question, what is an urban farm? While on one level it seems quite obvious—farming in a city—finding a workable definition is more difficult. Are community gardeners who don't sell their produce farmers? When does a city end and a suburb begin? Does growing landscape plants for sale constitute urban farming? If so, is every Home Depot and Lowe's actually an urban farm?

To answer these questions, we asked many of the farmers, gardeners, and community supporters from around the country how they would define urban farming. The answers were as diverse as the projects we profiled. Some considered urban farms places where communities take back their autonomy. Others focused on income generation. Still others concentrated on education. Perhaps the only "concrete" theme that draws all of these projects and people together is their *intention*. Everyone is striving to create a healthier community where people know their neighbors and have access to good food. I've pulled all these threads together and propose this working definition of urban farming: *An urban farm is an intentional effort by an individual or a community to grow its capacity for self-sufficiency and well-being through the cultivation of plants and/or animals.*

Building on this broad definition of urban farming, we can divide the projects profiled in *Breaking Through Concrete* into three simple categories.

URBAN FARMS: Either for-profit or nonprofit organizations that are growing produce, flowers, herbs, and/or animals within a city. These organizations have a paid staff that produces products for sale for a local market only.

COMMUNITY GARDENS: An individual or collection of individuals growing plants and/or animals on either public property or private property for their own consumption or to donate to the needy.

SCHOOL GARDENS: A garden located on a school campus that acts as a laboratory in conjunction with an academic class, a demonstration, or a source of food for the students. Farm to School programs, which link local farmers with school cafeterias and provide education to students, often work closely with school gardens to increase the consumption of local, fresh produce by students and school staff.

It is generally recognized that urban farms will never have the capacity to feed the entire population, although cities such as Havana, Cuba, are purportedly capable of supplying most of the fresh vegetables for the city's needs. Urban farms can, however, fill an important role in a broader effort to create a more sustainable and just food system. Phrases such as *agricultural urbanism* and *community food security* point to an intricate web of rural and urban farmers connected directly to local consumers and supported by government policy. Although these concepts fall outside the bounds of this book, urban farming is a critical player in the development of the future food system, not only in terms of production, but also, and more profoundly, in terms of advocacy and education.

The most important role of the urban farm is perhaps in the physical manifestation of the vision for a truly sustainable food system, and in the bringing together of the people who can make that happen. The urban farm is an ideal platform for generating dialogue among various parts of a community. Children learn what local fresh food tastes like and develop a desire for more. College students study the systems that control our food supply and get to put theory into practice by working on an urban farm. Parents have a place to purchase high-quality fresh, local food and see what a community could look like if it supported more local agriculture. Legislators witness a vivid example of good policy—community gardens thriving on every corner—as opposed to the end result of bad policy—more "food deserts" full of abandoned strip malls and unhealthy citizens without access to fresh food.

"Eat Your View" is a popular slogan in Europe. The idea is simple. When you buy food, you are voting. You are voting in favor of the way your purchase was produced, processed, distributed, and marketed. When you buy food from a local urban farm, you are increasing the demand for more local urban farms. Buy enough food and you will eventually be surrounded by farms. That means that urban farms are essentially the manifestation of consumers' desires to see a more just and sustainable food system—and to eat good food.

Why Are Urban Farms Appearing Right Now?

While there are thousands of different reasons to start an urban farm, a couple of themes seem to recur in almost all of the projects we profile in this book. Urban farms create a country that is less dependent on nonrenewable fossil fuels and has healthier citizens eating better food, communities with stronger economies and more jobs, and cities that provide their youth inspiration rather than desperation.

But why is all this happening right now? Perhaps the most significant shift that has occurred to create a fertile ground for urban farming is the view that cities should *not* be mindlessly consuming products made outside their borders, that they could be at least partially self-sufficient.

In her book *City Bountiful,* Laura Lawson has carefully documented the waves of interest in urban farming that have washed over America during the last century. These booms have usually accompanied significant financial stress or war. Municipalities and individuals have found urban farming to be both effective and affirming. Although it is possible that we are experiencing just another one of the booms Lawson cites, the diversity of projects currently thriving across the country points to deeper roots and perhaps a profound transformation in the way America views urban development and food systems.

The last decade has seen a huge increase in interest in local food, from celebrity chefs touting their fresh products to farmer's markets popping up around cities faster than mushrooms after a rain. Urban farms have obviously benefited directly from this interest. There is no better way to get fresh local food than from a farm down the street. But is this just a fad? Perhaps if this were occurring in isolation, the longevity of the interest could be expected to fade quickly. However, a couple of other trends are building that promise to change the foundation of our communities before this boom dissipates.

There is a growing recognition that our nation's public health is in peril due to what we are eating. The number of studies linking obesity and chronic disease to our diet expands exponentially each year. A consensus finally exists that public health advocates have to do more than address food-safety issues. What we are eating must change or we as a country will face significant negative impacts on our economy and even national security. With this understanding, there is little disagreement that increasing consumption of fresh fruits and vegetables is a simple solution, especially among children. Urban farms respond to this need perfectly.

Having children participate in the production of what they eat is a well-tested method for increasing their lifelong consumption of healthy foods. The idea is simple. If a child helps to grow something, he or she is more likely to experiment with that food. Once a child has eaten a certain food, he or she is more likely to try it again. And from there it's a small step to achieving a long-standing behavioral change—a change that began with putting a seed in the ground. So with the country's population steadily shifting to urban living, urban farms are positioned better than ever to address this simple education.

The recession of 2008 is perhaps an even more profound voice for urban farming than the public health correlation. Across the country, cities were quickly decimated by the burst of the housing bubble. Entire communities were vacated and unemployment rates skyrocketed. Major industries collapsed and municipalities that depended on them were left with limited alternatives. Urban farming is being seen as one of a few bright spots in an otherwise still somewhat bleak economic outlook. With relatively little capital investment, unemployed citizens can turn vacant land into something productive in a relatively short time.

The last trend that has given urban farming a big push is related to food safety. Over the last century, staggering numbers of family farms have been consolidated by corporations. Today, only a handful of corporations process the majority of our food, and an only slightly larger handful of farms produce that food. Because food prices have remained steady and few health problems have occurred, the public has paid little attention to this conglomeration. This all began to change in 2006, as one food-borne epidemic after another rocketed through the country. Everyone was quick to play a blame game and shirk responsibility. Large corporate farms blamed small organic farms for letting manure into the food systems. Small organic farms blamed factory farms for not providing adequate sanitation for their farm workers. No one seemed to notice that the entire food system is at fault. Urban farms have risen to the top of the food security debate as one of the only ways to secure safe food. If your food comes from down the street, you can inspect it yourself, and if there's a problem, it's easy to detect. On the other hand, large-scale food production, without massive increases in regulatory spending, prohibits any measurable means to ensure food is safe and to track a problem if one occurs. A diversified web of small local growers in close contact with their customers is a simple solution.

Who Is Farming?

One blazing hot day during the first summer I worked transforming a vacant lot into Jones Valley Urban Farm, I noticed a bunch of kids from the surrounding neighborhood climbing a tree tucked between a nearby shed and a fence. As a responsible organizational director, I went over to tell them that climbing in the tree was a liability and that they needed to go back across the street to the playground. As I got closer to the tree, I was shocked to see that their faces were covered with the blue juice of the mulberry. For years, these kids had been coming to this lot at this time each summer to feast on the mulberries. I was struck at how our efforts to cultivate a vacant lot into a food-production site had neglected to even notice this prolific weed tree growing quietly in the corner. The kids knew better.

Marilyn Nefer Ra Barber, who currently runs Detroit's D-Town Farm, is one of the many urban farmers we met across the country in the summer of 2010. Like many southerners over the last century, she moved north to Detroit in part to escape farm life. "Most of the people in Detroit left farms in the South," she says, "and they didn't want anything to do with the farm. Now we're almost at the point where we're forced into it again, but this time it's to gain the power to plant that seed and control your food. When you see it that way, you have to give the farm a second chance." Although Marilyn's experience with farming in the city is common from New York to Seattle, it is not the only story. When looking at who is farming in cities in America, it might be easier to ask who is *not* farming.

The urban farms we have profiled represent only a tiny sliver of the larger community of urban farmers in America today. You can literally find somebody from every demographic farming in the city. Marginalized African American communities are turning blighted vacant lots into community farms that bring power back into their local economies. Immigrant communities are blending their traditional agricultural techniques into sustenance and market gardening. Affluent communities are planting in backyards and church lawns, often donating the produce to feed residents of local shelters.

A growing trend among urban farmers goes back to an early incentive behind agriculture: to make a profit. Programs such as SPIN (small plot intensive farming) offer guidelines on how to turn small vacant lots into a viable income. The explosion of local farmer's markets is creating easier avenues for these farmers to sell their products directly to the consumer, and thereby actually make a living. In New Orleans, Marilyn Yank is experimenting with turning vacant corner lots into a neighborhood-supported farm. She supplies eight families with weekly produce from a tiny corner lot in downtown. She sees it as a simple experiment: "Can you make a living turning something wasted in the community into something healthy and productive? There's a formula that probably works. I'm trying to find out what it is."

One of the more profound distinctions of urban farmers is that they are rarely trained in agriculture or even come from an agricultural background. While nearly all conventional rural growers are "inheriting" an agricultural tradition, most urban farmers are driven by philosophical motives to better their community or make a living. Even though many nonprofits are developing training programs and academic institutions are beginning to offer courses in urban agriculture, we still have a long way to go before a system is in place to match the opportunities in urban farming with the supply of knowledgeable practitioners.

Where Are Urban Farms Occurring?

Urban farms are appearing in almost every corner of our cities, from strips along freeways to warehouse rooftops, from concrete planters next to front doors to entire city blocks. The spaces for urban farming are almost endless. The urban farms and community food projects profiled in this book are just a few examples of the hundreds of projects unfolding all over the country. We wanted to represent the breadth and width of what urban farming is in America in 2010. There are numerous wonderful projects that we do not mention, either because they declined our offer or because we did not have time to visit them or space to include them. It is our dream that future books that cover this same subject will be twice as long, and that this book will serve as a milestone, a measuring rod, for how far urban farming has progressed to date.

With just a bit of pruning, even kudzu and blackberries can have their place in this new American city. Maybe one day, every city in the South will have teams of goats foraging on kudzu instead of crews of men and women wielding gas-guzzling, fume-spewing weed eaters disrupting a peaceful summertime afternoon. And perhaps local restaurants will advertise food grown by the youth in the community or perfectly sweet jelly made from kudzu flowers. As long as cracks keep appearing in the concrete, anything is possible.

P-PATCH COMMUNITY GARDEN PROGRAM
SEATTLE, WASHINGTON

Dennis Moore, fifty-four, helped Antoinette Crotty dig out the blackberry-laced hillside that helped establish the Interbay P-Patch in 1974. Back then, as young twenty-somethings, Moore and his friends were fairly typical Seattleites—community-minded individuals with a do-it-yourself spirit—and the P-Patch community gardens popping up around the city represented that sensibility. Thirty-six years later, the P-Patch program is a national model for community gardening and a catalyst for progressive city policies that recognize and support urban agriculture in Seattle.

The P-Patch name derives from the first garden, begun in 1973 by a group of University of Washington students. They saw a patch of land that had lain fallow since its days as a truck farm in the 1920s and 1930s. The Picardo family owned the land and allowed the students to grow food and use the garden as a teaching space for area youth and other university students. A general back-to-the-land sentiment was running through much of the West Coast at the time, and Seattle, with its job losses following the 1967 to 1971 Boeing cuts, saw an opportunity for positive community growth via shared garden spaces. The city bought the original garden patch land from the Picardo family, and the concept for community gardens spread quickly on underutilized city lands, such as public right-of-ways, the ground beneath power lines, and abandoned lots. At the time Antoinette Crotty, Dennis Moore, and others were converting a blackberry patch into a P-Patch in the Interbay neighborhood, over ten community gardens were in the P-Patch organization. By 2010, there were seventy-three P-Patches farming twenty-three acres of city land.

The community garden infrastructure mimics the allotment gardens that have been popular in Britain and other countries for centuries. As opposed to an urban farm

Community members young and old tend the garden at the Interbay P-Patch, where, as at most P-Patches, there is often a waiting list for a plot.

that has a manager and a staff of employees or volunteers who collectively plan, sow, tend, and harvest the produce and flowers for market sales, the community garden model allots small beds to individuals who apply for a plot, pay a nominal fee (roughly fifty dollars per year), and adhere to a basic set of shared guidelines. Each bed is its own small farm, and the plot's owner can do what he or she wants with the food, though the majority use the produce for their respective households. In that way, the patch acts as a sort of surrogate garden for city dwellers who might not have the land or, as is common in Seattle, the sunlight to grow food.

Much of the longevity and success of the P-Patch program stem from its relationship with the city. The organization is housed within the city's Department of Neighborhoods. The P-Patch supervisor and five staff members manage gardens by maintaining the wait lists and registration, enforcing the rules of the farms (removing delinquent growers), cultivating volunteer leadership teams at gardens, networking the patches with food banks and charities, and working with communities that want to start new patches. The city created a fund in which volunteer hours worked on P-Patches are matched with monetary funding for maintenance, water, and supplies. The Neighborhood Matching Fund distributes roughly three million dollars a year to P-Patches throughout Seattle.

In addition to the financial boost the city provides, the P-Patches benefit greatly from the simple fact that they are recognized by the city and have a departmental place within city hall. That relationship gives Seattle's community gardens a voice in government, whereas most urban farms and community garden groups in other cities operate outside the political structure of their municipalities.

Andrea Petzel, a senior urban planner with the city of Seattle, has led an effort to recognize and define urban agriculture in the city. She identifies the P-Patch program as a major backbone to the city's overall understanding of and commitment to growing food in Seattle. In 2010, the city held a series of meetings and planning sessions to address urban agriculture and to begin creating policy.

Perhaps these meetings' most pivotal step was to define urban farming, which was deemed "growing food on a property and selling it." The planning office recognized a difference between an urban farm and a P-Patch or community garden, which is a shared space that gets treated like a park.

"The P-Patches kind of got us started in the right direction," Petzel says. "They are a recreational, community-building tool, and we need that grassroots foundation to

A benefit of community gardening sites is the chance for members to share knowledge and sometimes materials, such as the use of burlap sacks to curtail weeds.

inform and create a base for policy." The planning process was also important because it brought the grassroots people into the political world, which allowed them to see they have a role in policy creation. "We had everyone in those meetings: architects, farmers, hippies, developers, city planners," says Petzel. "It was a love fest among a wide variety of people."

The P-Patches and other community garden programs go beyond providing just a garden-away-from-home. They act as a "third place" within the participants' neighborhoods. Shared responsibilities ensure that collectivism is central to each P-Patch operation. Participants must volunteer a minimum of eight hours per year toward overall garden maintenance, such as weeding the pathways, turning the compost, mending fences or water lines, and, increasingly, collecting ripe produce for donation to local food banks. The Interbay P-Patch, for instance, donated twenty-seven thousand pounds of vegetables in 2009. Most of the food-bank vegetables are grown alongside gardeners' household produce, so that a small portion of each plot's yield goes to food banks. But some P-Patches, including Interbay, have cultivated dedicated sections of the property for food banks, with volunteer time spent tending and harvesting the crops.

The sense of inclusive support among the P-Patch growers and the city's needy has

Seattle's Interbay P-Patch
is a thirty-year-old site
in a busy residential area.

Thirty of Seattle's P-Patch gardens have programs for sharing produce with local food banks.

been around since the program's beginning. Dennis Moore has participated in every aspect of the P-Patches, from the first plantings on the Interbay site to the early roots of the donations to food banks and AIDS and cancer patients.

"Over thirty years, your garden means different things at different times," says Moore. "At first I was a starving college student, and if I didn't grow the produce in my garden, I wasn't eating."

Eventually, however, he began making food deliveries in the early 1980s, when the Interbay crew created the Chicken Soup Brigade to serve cancer and AIDS patients in Seattle. Moore enjoyed bringing the donations to the folks who couldn't leave their homes. "It's easy to think, 'Oh those people receiving the donation don't care; they're just getting free food.' But I saw that the patients really appreciated the freshness and quality of local produce. They immediately made the connection that what was happening was intentional—that the P-Patch gardeners were growing food for themselves, but were also growing it with the knowledge that they'd be sharing it with someone else."

18

The Interbay P–Patch borders a popular city golf course, and over the years, both the garden's members and the P–Patch organization have had to resist the advances of developers.

Moore has joined in the three fights to save the Interbay P-Patch from development, most recently from a group that wanted the land for condominiums. A golf course borders one side of the patch, and the site has only increased in real-estate value over the decades. The patch has been moved twice, but the garden continues to gain support, with a waiting list that increases every year.

For the last few years, Moore has grown flowers on his plot. They explode out of the soil and fan over the raised bed's border like frozen fireworks. Nowadays, Moore finds himself on the receiving end of the food donations. Although he still tends his flowers and volunteers on the patch's food-bank plot, he has become a client of the cancer and AIDS program he helped to start. So Moore benefits from the sharing, community spirit of the Interbay plot, from the P-Patch organization as a whole, and from the city of Seattle's willingness to officially recognize community gardening and bring it to the table of civic discussion.

The term *food security* gets used a lot these days, but Moore, who has traveled the length of the community-garden spectrum, from individual pioneer to donation recipient, prefers to call what's happening in Seattle with community P-Patches and throughout the country with the urban farm movement in general *food sovereignty*. He believes that phrase speaks to the root of it all, the organizational and individual *intent* of it all. It's the most important commonality of the entire urban agriculture movement, and it's a trait seen in every community gardener, urban farmer, volunteer, farmer's market shopper, and CSA (community supported agriculture) recipient throughout the country. The individual and community grassroots energy has been behind the movement for decades, but when cities follow Seattle's lead and begin to participate in and recognize the potential of urban agriculture, the horizons for the inclusive growth of urban farming expands. And as urban farming expands, the chances for a revitalized national food system grow.

ESTABLISHED: 1974.

SIZE: The seventy-three P-Patches throughout the city total 23 acres.

MISSION: To provide community gardening opportunities for the city of Seattle.

WHO'S IN CHARGE: Seattle's Department of Neighborhoods oversees the P-Patches; Rich MacDonald is the program supervisor.

SURROUNDING NEIGHBORHOOD: All neighborhoods of the city.

ZONING: Single-family residential.

FUNDING: The City of Seattle and the Neighborhood Matching Fund distribute about $3 million per year. The nonprofit P-Patch Trust provides tools and advocacy and supplies garden fees for P-Patches in low-income communities.

WHO EATS IT: The individual growers, plus the P-Patches contribute over 100,000 pounds of produce each year to Seattle food banks.

HOW TO Change Your City's Urban Agriculture Zoning Codes

With our food traveling greater distances to reach urban centers, city legislators have seen little reason to protect the capacity for food production in our backyards. City laws regarding such production have changed for the worse over the last fifty years, making most farming, especially raising livestock, illegal. The justification has been that food production is dirty and unsafe. Most people enjoy the benefits of a nonlocal food economy, so this change met with little resistance. If you can get mango-infused salmon in Chicago in January, what's the big deal?

But city halls are beginning to notice the urban farm movement and the clamor for action. Some of them, of course, are responding negatively. Others, however, are giving urban agriculture a seat at the proverbial table by writing new policy friendly to farmers and gardeners and livestock producers within the city limits.

The city of Seattle has become a poster child for urban agriculture. This shouldn't come as a surprise. The city boasts a climate like a greenhouse, and a vocal and dedicated percentage of the city's population never really moved away from the back-to-the-land movement that swept through in the 1970s, when the first P-Patches appeared on empty lots. For decades, the Pike Place Market has been the most popular tourist destination in the city. Imagine that: the strongest association made by tourists to a major city is a farmer's market full of local produce, flowers, and, of course, tossed fish.

Andrea Petzel, an urban planner with the city of Seattle, has been instrumental in pushing forward some of the Emerald City's latest initiatives aimed at bringing urban agriculture into the policy fold. Despite her success, she remains realistic: "It's important to remember that it took fifty years of making policy to get us where we are and it won't change course overnight. Our basic infrastructure prevents small and midsize farm distribution from succeeding."

But that's changing. As is often the case, it takes a major disaster to scare us out of the ease of the status quo. After Hurricane Katrina devastated New Orleans in 2005, cities across the country began questioning the logic of relying solely on a nonlocal food system. The City of Seattle officially started asking what would happen if a similar disaster occurred closer to home. That concern was well placed: Seattle is posed on one of the most active and potentially destructive earthquake-fault zones in the world and is surrounded by water on all sides. Local officials became conscious, perhaps for the first time, of the city's vulnerability, and they began to worry about not having enough food in an emergency. Quick research into food supplies and distribution systems available at any one time revealed that only about three days' worth of food would be on hand if disaster struck. That knowledge, coupled with the fact that the 2008 recession led to unprecedented waiting lists at the more than seventy city-managed P-Patch gardens, pushed local politicians to start looking at ways to make changes.

The Seattle City Council drafted a resolution called the Local Food Action Initiative. This followed a research project that showed how the city impacts the food system and how simple changes could improve that impact. They looked at "food as an organizing principle of government," which led to a number of alterations, the most significant of which was a change in zoning codes that removed all barriers to growing and selling food by citizens. Selling food grown in an individual's garden was deemed a business under the same rules that apply to a psychologist who sees patients in her home or a yoga instructor who leads yoga sessions in his backyard studio. Legislators made significant changes to policy that encouraged urban farming while still ensuring public health and safety.

The City of Seattle realizes that gardens, farms, and livestock are just one piece of the urban agriculture and food security puzzle; these new policies address production but not distribution, education, and public awareness, especially in underserved communities and "food deserts." Officials are now actively looking at big-picture issues, such as how to end hunger in Seattle. Staff in all the departments strategize at monthly meetings how to address food security throughout the city. Perhaps the city's involvement in restructuring the Seattle food system is just a reflection of a broader community waking up to the power that lies just under their feet. Regardless, the changes are growing and they are transferable to many other municipalities, big and small.

Tips on Working with Your Public Representatives to Help Change Zoning Codes

FIND A LEADER. Drastic changes can start with one person understanding the issue and being able to articulate a message to the public and to lawmakers.

BRAND THE MESSAGE. Provide education in a language policy makers understand.

START SMALL. Nonthreatening changes, such as supporting existing community gardens, can be great entry points into policy discussions. With these in place, you can look to bigger next steps.

ALTER ZONING. Current zoning doesn't need to be completely rewritten. Agriculture zoning can be overlaid on top of existing residential, commercial, or industrial areas. Legalizing the sale of products from the urban farm can be an additional component.

BE PATIENT AND PERSISTENT. Even in Seattle, politics prevented action from being taken on the Local Food Action Initiative for three years. A new mayor was elected in 2010, and the door opened to great changes.

SUPPORT OR START A FOOD POLICY ADVISORY COMMITTEE. Michael Pollan perfectly described the pitfalls of our municipal governments when he stated that there are no "Departments of Food." Instead, individuals must come together to craft recommendations to local government that officials can mold into policies that support a sensible, sustainable food system. Share the great policy templates available from the City of Seattle with your local legislature.

HOMELESS GARDEN PROJECT
SANTA CRUZ, CALIFORNIA

A field of Sonora wheat lends a constant sense of motion to a meadow above Central California's Pacific coast. The chest-high stalks that edge up to Santa Cruz's three-acre Homeless Garden Project (HGP) farm mirror those that have existed up and down the West Coast since the late eighteenth century, when Spanish missionaries arrived from Mexico. The heirloom grain makes an easy metaphor for HGP, which has established its own lineage through the sustainable farming world.

The twenty-year-old urban farm project has an intern program that plays out like the minor leagues of the urban farm movement. Edwin Marty learned at HGP; he went on to cofound Birmingham, Alabama's Jones Valley Urban Farm (and is the coauthor of this book). Amy Courtney cofounded Santa Cruz's Freewheelin' Farm, and Jered Lawson now runs the nearby Pie Ranch, on the San Mateo coast, and San Francisco's Mission Pie shop. Thus, HGP is not only a study in job creation and therapeutic horticulture for homeless members of society but also a testament to the long-term ripples that flow out of all urban farms and form the basis of the urban farm movement. The ripples are of agricultural knowledge, individual passion, and the savviness to make a small farm into a business. Although the vibrant greens, plump cucumbers, and fist-sized strawberries pulled from the HGP plots each day are more obvious, the impact that the project has on the lives of its employees and interns marks its greatest benefit. As Paul Glowaski, former farm manager, says, "The work we're doing here is largely for people we'll never meet."

The Homeless Garden Project's success story began with a small plot and a thousand donated herb plants tended by a few homeless men and women. The farm

Former farm director Paul Glowaski in a field of heirloom Sonora wheat.

now employs fourteen homeless trainees and provides weekly CSA shares to twenty-five members of the Santa Cruz community and to five social service organizations.

People sometimes shiver at the label "homeless," finding it demeaning. "Yeah, we get that sometimes," says Paul. "But at some point you've got to stand up and say, 'This is who we are, we're people.'"

The Homeless Garden Project is not a charity case. It grows beautiful organic produce to rival that found on any small farm in the country: deep shades of purple and maroon and green and yellow in the rainbow chard rows, artichoke stalks as tall as a man, kale, broccoli, squashes, lettuce, spinach, bok choy, lavender, wheat (they mill it to make the HGP pancake mix), and rows of cut flowers. It just so happens that homeless people given a chance at gainful employment for up to three years are the ones who are moving the plow, lining the irrigation tubes, harvesting the ripe produce, learning job skills, and enjoying the satisfaction of responsibility and community.

"We hit both sides," says Paul, a passionate man whose turquoise eyes almost tear up when he talks about the farm. "The progressives love us because we grow organic food and offer a social service, and conservatives love us because we provide job training."

By late May, the farm is about to go crazy. The strawberries lie fat and drunk in their sugary juices. The trainees crouch between the rows and pluck them off, chatting and laughing.

Robert Cochran arrived at the farm in the early spring of 2010, when he took a bus away from San Francisco and the bad scene he had fallen into there. He's lean and he smiles a lot. His voice is as deep as a blues singer's, but still all young and caramel smooth. He walks or takes the bus from the homeless shelter, and he saves his money from the hourly farm wage (which he earns by working twenty hours a week, Tuesday through Friday, 9:00 a.m. to 2:00 p.m.). His training covers much more than just tending to the garden. Trainees participate in courses that range from plant pathology to résumé building to meditation.

"Right now, it's like I'm starting over," says Robert. "And that's exactly what I wanted to do. Before, I never had anything I actually earned. Never got to watch something grow and prosper. With this, if I start something, if I plant something in that bed and ten years later someone else is working on that same plant, I can know I helped do that. It's something that I've finished and it gives me a great deal of hope and confidence in myself."

HGP illustrates an example of a classic urban farm dilemma. Many of the urban farm projects around the country do not have a mission strictly focused on producing food. Work training and education farms like the Homeless Garden Project straddle the line between being a farm that sustainably grows marketable vegetables and fruits and being a safe place that provides a social service to city residents, frequently people on the fringe of society who likely do not come to the job with agricultural training. HGP must grow quality produce to be legitimate and avoid the pitfall of becoming "just another good cause" in which sympathetic townspeople buy products that are priced above their value. But the farm must also prioritize the needs of its employees and adhere to its mission of providing a service to them.

"Some of these trainees are dealing with serious issues surrounding mental health, addiction, and physical pain," says Paul. "Sometimes my goal of harvesting the vegetables and getting them to the CSA members doesn't always mesh with the day-to-day realities of someone who's homeless and living in a shelter."

Darrie Ganzhorn has been the executive director of HGP for almost the project's entire twenty years. She works in the gift shop in downtown Santa Cruz, where trainees make wreaths and candles and other value-added farm goods during the

Early morning at the
Homeless Garden Project
in Santa Cruz.

winter. Darrie has worked with hundreds of trainees and has seen some move on to success and others slide back down the wrong side of life. Since 2000, her records show, two-thirds of the trainees have become more stable in some way. Darrie recognizes the vagueness of measuring a *sense* of stability, but she also knows how damaged the trainees can be on arrival at the farm after years of living on the streets and, for some, not receiving the medical and psychiatric help they need.

"There are many definitions of success," she says. "I believe that changes such as beginning to receive disability payments for a chronic illness, seeking mental health support for a long-untreated condition, or reconnecting with family can be a huge leap forward, even though it doesn't sound like much to some of us. And one-third of our trainees have moved into employment."

HGP doesn't call itself a horticultural therapy project. Leigh Anne Starling, a horticultural therapist and HGP board member, describes the difference between horticultural therapy and what HGP provides its trainees: "Horticultural therapy is the engagement of the client in horticultural activities facilitated by a trained horticultural therapist. It takes place in a rehabilitative and/or health-care setting utilizing plant-based activities monitored by therapists trained in both horticulture and working with people with a disability."

The farm managers at HGP aren't trained in clinical therapy, so the farm program cannot qualify as horticultural therapy treatment. That said, Leigh Anne recognizes the potential for positive rehabilitation, whether it be mental or physical, in farming. "What's healing about the work at the Homeless Garden Project is that plants mirror people and there is so much to be learned there. People on an instinctual level have nurturing needs. We all have a need to take care of something. So a person can fulfill his or her unmet nurturing needs with the plant in a safe relationship."

Darrie calls it therapeutic horticulture, and there's no denying the healing taking place within the secure, productive space of the farm. To Darrie, therapy and recovery, in addition to hard-won job skills, are intrinsic in a farm. "Someone once said farming can't be therapy, that therapy requires full-time attention to the human needs, and horticulture requires the same for plants," says Darrie. "Perhaps there is some truth to that, but I like being in that space, right there in the middle where there's a tension between the needs of the plant and the needs of the person.

"It's like the tension between training and production; there's synergy there, too. The high standard for our production quality is the best approach. There's a training involved in doing the best and doing as much as you can. And that kind of training works. It takes a while to settle in, which is why we offer a program somewhat longer than traditional training programs."

Santa Cruz, due in part to its recent high-priced real-estate boom and emergence as a prime relocation town for young and retired professionals, finds .9 percent of its population homeless, just below the U.S. average of .96 percent. Like any population, the homeless men and women are a diverse lot, with differences that go far deeper than ethnicity, age, or gender. Darrie has to consider the variables of background when hiring her trainees.

"We use a grid of three criteria when hiring: readiness to make change, ability to contribute, and need for the project. So we get a diverse range of people—not in skin color, though there's that, of course, but in terms of their experience with homelessness."

Although it can be stressful to produce great food on a timely schedule for the farm's CSA, the act of farming, especially with the physically challenging French-intensive method used at HGP, provides a natural lesson. The patience and dedication required to see a plant grow from a seed have healing and teaching qualities that can play a pivotal role in regaining emotional stability and confidence.

"Food has incredible meaning for survival," says Darrie. "It's so needed and tangible and there's such satisfaction in planting a seed and seeing it grow. You see results.

"People say that when they're weeding they're throwing away the bad thoughts. They see the clean row in front of them, and this pile of bad stuff off to the side. Farming and providing food for people is an honorable thing and it's very healing."

Friday's full day of harvesting that precedes the weekly CSA shares distribution has just ended. Paul gushes with pride over HGP's products, from the vegetables and fruits to the honeys, jams, and wreaths sold in the shop. He also talks about his own role in the big picture of urban farms and the role of his generation of twenty- to thirty-year-olds. He believes that the new crop of farm entrepreneurs brings a different outlook to the nonprofit world than the one established by that of their parents. He sees the nonprofits of the future relying less on grants and donations and more on a sustainable, profitable business approach. Paul is part of the ripple effect of the HGP. Late in 2010, he moved on to start his own farm nearby, setting himself three goals: to grow produce of high quality, provide himself with a living wage, and improve his community through the input of healthy, fresh food. He and Darrie agree that HGP has altered the perspective on nonprofits, at least in Santa Cruz.

"People from town walk into the shop sometimes just because it's a homeless shop and something they might want to support," Darrie says. "But they see the wreaths, for instance, and they are totally wowed. It's changing the stereotype of a homeless training project, and we're hitting the economic leg of the triple bottom line."

The triple bottom line means success at the ecological, social, and economic levels of a business. It's the idea that profit and economic goals don't have to be left out of a social and environmental business or program, and vice versa. It's easy to see businesses that miss the ecological and social part. But many nonprofits, especially

production urban farms, no longer want to rely on fund-raisers and grants. They want and need to hit the economic corner of the triangle. Independence and vitality will help a younger generation achieve success on all three levels.

The sun takes its time setting and the wind is cold. The trainees have left the farm. Paul is still on the site. This is his time to relax. He says that at this crepuscular hour, just after the sun has fallen but the sky remains softly bright, the farm reveals itself in a brief moment of subdued colors when everything alive is moving, either coming or going.

HGP offers internships to young farmers, some of whom have gone on to create small farm projects of their own.

ESTABLISHED: 1990.

SIZE: 3 acres.

MISSION: To bring together people in the beauty and security of a certified organic garden, to practice and teach principles of economic and ecological sustainability through classes and hands-on experience, and to provide homeless men and women job training and transitional employment.

WHO'S IN CHARGE: Executive director (Darrie Ganzhorn), who supervises five staff, fourteen trainees, and two to four interns.

SURROUNDING NEIGHBORHOOD: The edge of Santa Cruz's built environment, with new condominiums that include market-rate and low-income housing to one side and coastal land preserve to the other.

ZONING: General industrial.

FUNDING: Foundation grants, 39 percent; individual donations, 29 percent; earned income, 23 percent; corporate donations, 5 percent; government funding, 4 percent. Earned income has decreased over the years, due mainly to increased staff salaries.

WHO EATS IT: CSA members and five social service organizations (Women's Crisis Support, Santa Cruz AIDS Project, Independent Living Program, Beach Flats Community Center, Live Oak Family Resource Center).

HOW TO Grow Good, Safe Food

There's really only one way to know your food is safe: grow it yourself. The next best approach is to know who grows your food, to see it being grown, and to know the story of organic farming. The term *organic* is becoming increasingly commodified and, surprisingly, more and more difficult to decipher. The urban farm offers a wonderful way to know your farmer and know where and how your food is being cultivated.

It's no coincidence that most of the urban farms prospering across America are using organic farming techniques. Whether they tend tiny community garden plots or acre-wide urban fields, almost all urban farmers operate on the principle that synthetic fertilizers and pesticides are negatively impacting our food system. While a wide spectrum of motivations exists for "going organic," anyone who falls into the organic category agrees that food production should be a healthy enterprise.

Most urban farms are growing food either to donate or to sell directly to consumers, such as at farmer's markets or via CSAs, and those customers and recipients expect clean, sustainably grown food. The phrase *clean food* implies that no synthetic chemicals—fertilizers, pesticides, or herbicides—were used in cultivation. But the food is not always necessarily organic, or rather certified organic, a label that refers specifically to the National Organic Program of the United States Department of Agriculture (USDA). As the scale of urban farming continues to grow, more and more urban farms are looking to sell their products to a wider market, and they know that securing the "certified organic" label can help them do that.

Until around 2000, the term *organic* was used loosely to refer to anyone farming without man-made chemicals, and many states had certification boards that could verify farmers' claims. The certification helped farmers sell their harvests by assuring customers that they were getting a "better" product—a product that justified a slightly higher price than what its nonorganic equivalent fetched.

But because each state had a different definition, and some states had none at all, significant confusion arose around what was legally organic. The USDA got involved and put together the National Organic Program (NOP), which provides consumers with a standard for understanding the term and helps farmers sell their products on a larger scale.

There was a robust debate about the labeling and much dissent. Many small growers felt that the entire reason they were farming organically was being diluted to allow farmers engaged in large-scale production to use the term *organic*. Many customers were concerned about the practices that were allowed under the new definition. For example, at one point the use of sewage sludge was permitted under the organic label.

The USDA now has the authority to fine farmers if they claim to be organic but do not have certification. Since the USDA's adoption of the organic label, numerous alternative certifications have appeared, such as "naturally grown" and "clean food." These labels attempt to reduce the bureaucracy of certification for small growers but still give them a way to communicate with customers about the quality of their products. Although such labeling efforts are effective for marketing, none of them can assure you that the system from which your food comes is a safe, healthy one. Only seeing the system for yourself provides that peace of mind.

Reasons to "Go Organic"

MARKETING. Many of the best urban farmer's markets require growers to have an organic certification. Cultivate Kansas City (page 67) requires that the growers they train use organic techniques because their primary market requires certification.

AFFORDABILITY AND EFFICIENCY. Utilizing local, organic inputs like compost, which an urban farm can often produce itself, is a more affordable, efficient option than buying fertilizer. Plus, the improved soil typically results in increased production.

POLICY. Some urban farms are required to use organic techniques as part of the agreement that put the land into their hands. For example, Fairview Gardens (page 39) farms organically because provisions in the original land trust that protected the property from development stipulate it.

SAFETY. Using organic farming techniques exposes farm workers to fewer dangerous synthetic chemicals, reduces negative impacts on soil and water quality, and poses fewer health concerns to the consumer.

PHILOSOPHY. Organic farming is much more than just a farmer deciding *not* to use this synthetic chemical fertilizer or that herbicide. It's a way to hit the triple bottom line of social, economic, and environmental sustainability. Darrie Ganzhorn, director of the Homeless Garden Project, sums up many urban farmers' thoughts: "In our vision, sustainability, beauty, and safety all have a place in building community and creating justice, or you could call it harmony."

How to Put Organic Farming into Practice

Everything you do to produce food should regenerate the natural resources used, not deplete them. What you choose to feed your soil and plants makes the difference.

USE FERTILIZERS SELECTIVELY. Avoid synthetic fertilizers, which deplete the soil over time. Instead, use compost, which recycles nutrients. You can also use fish emulsion (ground fish parts), a by-product of the fishing industry that is a particularly good source of nitrogen fertilizer.

AVOID PESTICIDES. Roughly 98 percent of all insects are beneficial to the environment. That means you should never spray a synthetic chemical that kills "unselectively." Instead, cultivate a balanced system where the beneficial insects, such as ladybugs and wasps, eat the pests. If an outbreak of a pest insect occurs, use a physical, biological, or chemical organic insecticide to reduce the population of that specific insect. Visit the USDA's National Organic Program Web site for a list of relevant products.

AVOID HERBICIDES. While synthetic chemicals can effectively control most weed problems, the true cost of their use to our environment is staggering, with excess chemicals ending up negatively impacting our aquatic ecosystems. Organic farmers rely on continuously rotating crops to ensure the soil is regularly cultivated, which kills the weeds. Explore some of the new organic herbicides, too, which are showing positive results.

FAIRVIEW GARDENS AND THE CENTER FOR URBAN AGRICULTURE
SANTA BARBARA, CALIFORNIA

Buried in the suburbs of Santa Barbara, California, rows of avocados, peaches, plums, and citrus stretch toward the deep blue Southern California sky. Interplanted among the rows are vibrant seasonal and annual vegetables. Lacinato kale and Bright Lights Swiss chard poke out of rich, fertile soil. Chickens stroll the grounds looking for grubs and find hidden pockets in which to lay their speckled or blue eggs.

Unlike most other urban farms in American, Fairview Gardens is unique not so much because of what it has become over the years as for what it has not become over the years. It is the oldest organic farm in California and was saved from the fate of most other farms in the area through the development of the Center for Urban Agriculture and a conservation easement. Without these two events, Fairview would look just like the cul-de-sac suburban developments that surround the farm for miles in every direction.

Walking across the farm, manager Toby McPartland says, laughing, "We farm in a glass house." The walls separating it from the suburban housing tracts enclose the farm on nearly all sides, creating an island of agriculture within a sea of modern American development. The public library is on one corner and the headquarters for the local school district is across the street. In many ways, the neighborhood could be described as a perfectly planned community. The residents have their safe streets, nearby commercial areas, a school, and their food source. Unfortunately, it wasn't planned this way.

Invariably, a tension arises when any farm project moves onto a vacant lot within an existing neighborhood. As with any somewhat radical change (and transforming a rubble-strewn lot into a plot that boasts rows of vegetables, a scattering of chicken coops, and a staff of farmers indeed marks that kind of change), the community

Javier Gomez, one of Fairview's resident farmers, holds a black rock chicken, one of the many resident hens that provide eggs to the farm and surrounding community.

Transplanting seed-
lings instead of seeding
directly in the field is one
way Fairview Gardens
maximizes its yield and
increases sales income.

must anticipate a period of growing pains until both sides—the new farmers and the established residents—get to know one another and begin to create realistic expectations for the brand-new relationship. Fairview's situation tells the inverse of that common urban farm story.

In Fairview's case, the farm came *first*. It has been on this same plot of land since 1895. Over time, the houses and building codes and community guidelines and neighborhood and city committees came to the farm's edge, not vice versa. It might be assumed that Fairview's century-old presence would secure it a modicum of precedence for operating a farm. But civic unrest and misunderstanding from neighbors—over tractor noise, chickens, and even the insects and pests typical to any farm—raised concerns from the new suburban residents. While kids in the neighborhood have always cherished their relationship with the Fairview chickens, their parents have had major issues with the roosters.

The solution to the battle between farm and suburb was the creation of the nonprofit Center for Urban Agriculture, which focused on securing land conservation easements and historical designation. From there, Fairview has had to work with the city to gain approval and permits for such farm activities as raising fifty or so chickens. But Fairview hit a wall with most efforts to conform to city policies because no precedents exist in the city books for an urban farm operating on a small scale. The fact that the historic farm has no historic safety net in the coding and zoning of the city-planning books marks a frustrating irony in the Fairview story. The permit process for chickens, for example, requires obtaining a commercial poultry operation permit that costs ten thousand dollars. Such a fee will never make sense on Fairview's scale of operation. "The rules are drawn up for giant farms, and there's little room for accommodating an operation on our scale," Toby says. "We're just trying to feed our community."

Community relations have improved since the early days of suburban growth. Santa Barbara residents can be characterized as interested in local agriculture and business and supportive of environmentally and socially progressive endeavors. And the Goleta Valley, in which Santa Barbara resides, is one of the most ideal places in America to grow food: the climate and soil are perfect for producing a wide variety of products with few naturally occurring problems. Yet farmland is disappearing at an alarming rate. Fairview is the voice for preserving what remains. Michael Ableman, founder of the Center for Urban Agriculture, helped create a model land trust that ensures Fairview will be a farm forever. The trust, which was the first of its kind, requires that the land always remain a working organic farm and that education be an ongoing component.

Toby McPartland is dedicated to keeping Fairview a productive farm. "We aren't farming for 'production.' We're farming for profits. I sit down every year and decide how much we want to make and then create a crop plan that enables us to do that. We have a finance committee that meets once a month, including professors from the University of California at Santa Barbara, that helps make changes to ensure we put together a profitable example."

Fairview exemplifies how an urban farm can create demand for high-quality, locally grown organic products cultivated on a small scale and supplement that market further with supplies from larger, more rural growers. As in so much of the nation's food-production debate, a tension exists between Fairview's desire to produce a diversity of food that the local community wants and that is healthy for the land and the temptation to use the land for less intensive, more profitable (for now) monocropping. Toby explains, "I'm doing a profit-and-loss study on each crop to figure out what's the best thing for us to grow. We've seen that kale is a really profitable crop because there's high demand and we can harvest off the same plant ten to twelve times in a season. We call it a cut-and-come-again crop."

Toby and the Fairview staff are developing relationships with local growers so that

Santa Barbara's Fairview Gardens was a thriving farm long before the arrival of the suburbs that now surround it.

Fairview can focus on growing high-dollar specialty crops and then buy other crops from rural farmers. This allows them to keep their CSA members happy with a diverse amount of food and at the same time not lose money on vegetables that don't make sense at such a small scale. The end goal is to increase the economic security for the regional farmers while still providing a diversity of products to local customers. "We're looking at whether all our markets need to be so diverse or if we can focus on some niche crops to make more money," says Toby. "For instance, we're growing wonderful Spanish Padrón peppers specifically for local Hispanic restaurants. We're providing strawberries to the district schools. The key is figuring out what's the most profitable thing to grow for a farm our size."

This model illustrates a potentially powerful way to make urban farms across the country relevant to a broader spectrum of the community. There's no way urban farms can produce enough food to feed everyone. But they can create demand for locally grown products and supply a certain portion of that market. The balance between education and production is the crucial part of the model and something Fairview's newest director, Mark Tollefson, takes seriously. "We are working on an apprenticeship program so that people from all over the country can come here to learn how to farm," explains Mark. "We can teach the economic viability of small-scale farming. But to do that, we need entrepreneurs now like we've never needed them before, and the only way we're going to get them is by training them."

Fairview provides a classic example of how urban farms put the entrepreneurial intellect to the test. Although there is tremendous support for Fairview in the community, the agricultural system is not built for local connections. For instance, a major challenge for Fairview comes from Santa Barbara's high real-estate costs. The salaries of the farm's staff cannot keep up with the city's cost of living. Farm labor is an often overlooked aspect of urban farming. At Fairview, the entire farm labor staff comes from one extended family that originally emigrated from Mexico. The core members have been working this land for over twenty years, and they know it like the back of their hand. For years, the family has lived in temporary housing on the farm due, in part, to the high real-estate prices in the surrounding community. Santa Barbara is one of the most expensive places to live in the country, and it would be virtually impossible for a farm laborer to pay rent, much less buy a house. Unfortunately, the City of Santa Barbara forced Fairview to remove their temporary housing a few years ago, putting the entire farm in jeopardy. In a compromise with the city, the workers

currently live in yurts on the farm. The Fairview board is drafting plans to build model farm labor housing.

This situation points to an obvious relationship that doesn't currently exist: the price of food should be reflected in the value of the land. An economically balanced relationship would enable farmers to live in the communities they feed. But because our food is radically subsidized on many levels, land values have nothing to do with how productive the land actually is. And thus Fairview represents a powerful educational symbol for the country's last half century of growth, which has seen much of our nation's most productive farmland given over to suburban housing.

If we want to have a diverse, safe, and resilient food system, the farmland surrounding cities must be preserved and valued. For Mark Tollefson, it all starts with connecting to the next generation. "I've worked with thousands of high-school students in the last decade and talked with them about how they see the world. Unfortunately, they're saying two things: 'the problems are too big, and there's nothing I can do about them.' I can't accept that this is our future. As the father of two small children, I have to confront the question of what we can do to move forward. Can we give the next generation of children hope?"

Fairview and the Center for Urban Agriculture are working to become a national training center for urban agriculture. Mark envisions youth from all over the country coming to the historic farm to learn the basics of food production, from young adults serious about operating a farm business to young children eating strawberries they have just picked by hand. "We need to have kids laughing on the farm. I'd like to hear

THE CENTER FOR URBAN AGRICULTURE AT
FAIRVIEW GARDENS

Fairview Gardens operates a roadside produce stand that generates much-needed revenue and is a valuable resource for the nearby community.

the music of laughter from children all the time. Once they understand the place of the farm in their lives on that level, everything else takes care of itself."

ESTABLISHED: Fairview in 1895; the Center for Urban Agriculture in 1997.

SIZE: A 12-acre urban farm and a 25-acre suburban farm.

MISSION: To demonstrate the economic viability of small-scale urban agriculture while providing education to farmers, policy makers, and the local community.

WHO'S IN CHARGE: Executive director (Mark Tollefson) supervised by a board of directors.

SURROUNDING NEIGHBORHOOD: Suburban tract homes, a public library, and the school district headquarters.

ZONING: Commercial. Zoned as a land trust to ensure that it remains a farm.

FUNDING: Earned income (produce sales and education programs), private donations, fund-raising events, and public and private grants.

WHO EATS IT: 250 CSA members, customers at local farmer's markets and an on-site farm stand, and various institutions, including local schools, through wholesale distribution.

HOW TO Plant Perennial Fruit Trees in the City

City horticulture departments are fond of planting non-fruit-bearing fruit trees. It's a win-win situation: the trees provide the same beauty as a fruit-bearing tree—amazing flush of spring blossoms and shade in the summer—without all that pesky fruit litter to clean up in the fall. This is, of course, absolute heresy to the urban farmer. Why on earth would you intentionally plant something that *wouldn't* feed people?

A group of volunteers in Asheville, North Carolina, got inspired twelve years ago to turn an old landfill on parks and recreation land into an edible park. The George Washington Carver Edible Park now hosts over forty varieties of fruit trees and is an amazing example to cities around the world of how easy it can be to turn wasted urban space into something beautiful and productive. The park provides free food to whoever wants it and connects communities, and kids especially, with their food system. What's best is that it costs about the same as maintaining a traditional park.

In Santa Barbara, Doug Hagensen helps run a nonprofit called Backyard Bounty that scavenges unwanted fruit from backyards, public spaces, and farms to redistribute to the hungry. "We've got lots of hungry people in our community," Doug explains. "Every city has people not getting enough food, and especially not getting the right kind of food. We're just trying to connect the dots." Organizations like Backyard Bounty are popping up in cities across the country.

Fruit trees in the city can also be a simple way to make our food system more efficient and improve the health of low-income residents. In New Orleans, for example, the mirliton (chayote) tree has grown for centuries, hanging over sidewalks and shading backyards with its dense canopy. The meaty gourd fruit has long been used as a rich filler in many New Orleans recipes, a readily accessible nutritional bonus without a price tag.

While fruit trees in parks and public spaces make a lot of sense, there's also a good reason to add them to the mix of an urban farm. Many urban farms are struggling to discover a formula for profitability. That includes nonprofit farms, like Fairview Gardens, which routinely rely on sales of fruits and vegetables for a portion of their annual revenue. But even though locally produced organic fruit is in high demand in urban areas, there are some things that should be taken into consideration before planting fruit trees.

Toby McPartland, farm manager at Fairview Gardens, tends to the dozen or so varieties of fruiting plants on the urban farm and has some strong opinions. "We have a system called alley cropping. We plant short fruit trees in rows, and then we grow annuals between the rows. It's a simple way of getting the most production out of a small piece of land."

While everyone who has ever visited Fairview can attest to the beauty of the system, it has some drawbacks. "People really connect to the aesthetics of these fruit trees, and that's one of the great things we've got here. It's a big part of our mission. But we're also a production farm that's working on models of efficiency."

Although it might not be as "sexy," Toby speculates that rows of radishes would be more profitable than the apples or pears. "The fruit trees produce for only a short season and then they just sit there taking up space," says Toby. "Radishes can be replanted over and over again to keep generating income. For instance, we yanked out the asparagus this year. It just wasn't paying its rent."

Part of Fairview's challenge is that it has changed its marketing plan over the years, but the perennial fruit trees have stayed the same. When the trees were planted twenty years ago, Fairview's CSA had 50 members and the trees provided a small quantity of fruit to each member. Now, the CSA has 250 members and the trees can't possibly provide enough for everyone. "We need to have fewer varieties and more of each variety," explains Toby. "I would like to have less of the alley cropping and a little more intensive production. We don't want to be a big monocropper, but we do want to be efficient."

While the scale and diversity of fruit crops are a challenge at Fairview, fruit trees can still provide some great pluses for an urban farm, for housing developments, and for city parks departments. They require less labor in general than annual crops, and they don't need to be weeded as often.

Five Urban-Friendly Fruit Trees

FIG. Fig trees require little maintenance and produce a large quantity of great-tasting, nutritious fruit that can fetch up to a dollar each at a local market. They prefer rich, well-drained soil but can survive in a wide range of soils, making them perfect for urban planting. Prune them in the winter to keep the fruit reachable without a ladder. Fig trees prosper in USDA Plant Hardiness Zones 5 and above, which make them a good choice for most U.S. cities.

POMEGRANATE. Somewhat prickly pomegranate plants are more like a bushy shrub than a tree. They make great hedges for bordering a farm plot and produce plenty of nutritious fruit at the same time. The plants like the sun, are drought tolerant, and do not like wet soil, so plant in raised beds, if possible. Pomegranates prosper in USDA Plant Hardiness Zones 7 through 10, which restricts their cultivation to cities with mild winters.

MULBERRY. Often considered a weed tree, the mulberry yields fruits that are just as tasty as blackberries. It is tolerant of drought, pollution, and poor soil—ideal qualities for an urban fruit tree. Prune to keep the fruit easier to harvest. Mulberry trees prosper in USDA Plant Hardiness Zones 7 through 10, so, like the pomegranate, will do best in an urban setting with a mild winter.

ASIAN PEAR. These trees don't need fertile soil and give shade to leafy crops like lettuce, protecting them from the searing summer sun, making them perfect for an urban farm. They are resistant to most common fruit-tree diseases and produce wonderfully crisp, delicious fruits. Asian pears can prosper in USDA Plant Hardiness Zones 5 and above, making them suitable for cultivation in most U.S. cities.

KIWIFRUIT. A woody vine that produces nutritious, refreshing fruits, the kiwifruit tree needs a sturdy trellis to support its considerable weight during the growing season. To ensure adequate fruiting, plant male and female vines in close proximity to each other and keep the soil moist. New varieties can prosper in USDA Plant Hardiness Zones 4 and above, making them ideal for most U.S. cities.

DENVER URBAN GARDENS
DENVER, COLORADO

It's hard to miss the East Thirteenth Street Garden on a summer afternoon. The whole neighborhood around Yosemite and East Colfax streets seems to move faster and brighter and freer than most city blocks. Teenagers swerve through the neighborhood on BMX bikes, residents jaywalk across streets, and kids splash in the creek next to the sidewalk. Clothes hang to dry on the balconies of the blocky, plain apartment buildings that are surrounded by parking lots.

Amid so much human movement and urbanity, there's a patch of green bordered by a chain-link fence. While the vegetation softens the look relative to the nearby pavement, the commotion and color of the neighborhood remain the same inside as they do on the streets. Women wrapped in red-and-gold-seamed shawls and long, flowing dresses crouch to weed small beds of baby shoots. Kids sit under a tree sucking mangoes on a stick, sold by a woman with a pushcart on the sidewalk. Men are here, too. They water and weed and chat with one another.

Few people speak English, but twenty-eight-year-old Abukar Maye does. He's a Somali Bantu who spent ten years in a Kenya refugee camp. He works security at a Hyatt Hotel and lives "with Americans" in a neighborhood on the other side of town. He embodies the enthusiasm exhibited by the men, women, and children in the garden.

"We come to the gardens because we want to do something that reminds us of Africa," he says. "If I am in Somalia, I am going to make a lot of fruit. To have a garden is fun. The food is fresh, and it's better than staying inside the house."

The garden was started with help from Denver Urban Gardens (DUG), a nonprofit that began reclaiming vacant lots and park space for gardens in 1985. They don't run the projects. Rather, the organization acts as a resource for tools, teaching, land

A local resident stands in one of the community gardens that share space with the working production farm at DeLaney Farm, one of the scores of plots that Denver Urban Gardens has helped found.

access, and planning support. Except at its own working farm, known as DeLaney Farm, where a DUG employee manages the daily operations, the DUG staff let the gardens and the people do the work of growing food and building community.

East Thirteenth Street Garden is in the middle of a neighborhood of modest houses and apartment buildings that has become home to many refugees. Many of the residents arrived from Somalia in the early 2000s, after spending years in Kenyan refugee camps. When the refugees are cleared to immigrate to America, the United States State Department places them in various cities, ideally where they have friends or family and where a strong social service network exists, in this case the Mercy Housing Authority. The refugees often end up living in tight-knit communities that form a natural safety net.

Because the majority of the refugees worked as farmers or at least grew fruits and vegetables for their households in their homelands, the community farm becomes a gathering place where they immediately feel comfortable. There is soil to tend, food to harvest, and, most important, neighbors with shared history, language, and culture. The simple corner-lot garden becomes the "third place"—that essential piece of daily life that defines the community outside one's home or one's workspace. In the East Thirteenth Street Garden, customs and etiquettes from another continent can operate, while beyond the garden's fence, the immigrants must adapt to a new set of rules and expectations.

A community must be inclusive to survive. At East Thirteenth Street, a new influx of Bhutanese immigrants joined the Somali Bantu in 2009. They, too, wanted to gather over the growing of food, so they now share the garden's parcel with the Somali Bantu. The relationship between the two groups can be strained, as two distinct cultures struggle to communicate different customs and boundaries in the same plot. Tension can arise anywhere people gather in a space of shared ownership; it's the nature of community. The Somali Bantu and Burmese Karen groups have worked together, with DUG, the Trust for Public Land, and Denver's Department of Recreation, to design an extensive park and garden space on their vacant block. The planning process brought the two communities, with planners and architects, to one table and it proved successful. On the whole, Denver's garden network offers a living example of how the open community garden can bring people together and become a place of cultural identity and ownership, creating roots that run deeper than those of the food being grown in the soil.

DUG recently worked with the Colorado School of Public Health on a formal study to answer the question, do community gardens really enhance the communities and do they reach a broad audience? The finding of the six-year study, called Gardens Growing Healthy Communities, was a resounding yes, and DUG's farm and community garden projects provide anecdotal evidence. In 2010, DUG supported the construction of its one-hundredth community garden. The garden plots engage people from every corner of the city—the suburbanites at DeLaney Farm in formerly rural Aurora, African and Asian refugees in East Colfax, school students at the Peace Garden in Sunny Side, and upper-middle-class professionals in Rosedale.

Heather DeLong is program and outreach coordinator for DUG's DeLaney Farm. This historic thirty-acre farm sits at the end of the classic progression of urban development, from Denver's dense city core to industrial warehouses and trucking yards to big-box retail centers and the modern-day suburban house farm in once-rural Aurora. At DeLaney Farm, the beige, paved America opens to green grasses, faded white farm buildings, and row crops colored by a few individuals weeding, harvesting, or watering.

Heather manages the DUG outreach program that works with the Women, Infants, and Children (WIC) social service, a federal program that stretches DUG's reach beyond DeLaney Farm's immediate community. WIC clients have three options to take advantage of the farm and its fresh food. The women who join DUG's WIC Program can work an hour at the farm on one or both of two weekdays on which staff are available

The DeLaney Farm combines community garden plots with a production farm that supplies fresh food for a CSA and outreach programs.

Sunset over the Kingman Park Rosedale Community Garden, located in a solidly upper-middle-class neighborhood of Denver.

to help them. After an hour of weeding or planting, the women take home a share of vegetables. DUG also sends staff to the WIC clinics to offer recipes and instructions for cooking healthy food. Finally, the DeLaney Farm's weekly farm stand, like the DUG-sponsored youth farm stands around the city, offers card machines that accept the new Denver food stamps, known as SNAP cards (Supplemental Nutrition Assistance Program).

Faatma Mehrmanesh manages the day-to-day operations at DeLaney Farm. She rides a John Deere tractor in style. Her long hair is bundled up and held in place beneath a woven cloth hat. Turquoise headphones let her rock to the tractor's slow roll over the soil. She's preparing the plot for its first planting; the growing season starts late at the base of the Rocky Mountains.

"Even some of my friends just drive by and think this is a site that's about to be developed," says Faatma. "They don't even really know we're here, growing food every day. We have a DUG community garden on the front side, and we grow on the adjacent

At the East Thirteenth
Street Garden, two
Somali Bantu youth enjoy
mangoes on a stick.

three acres behind the garden. We have seventy full CSA shareholders. All in all, we provide food to about five hundred families, between the CSA and the partnerships with WIC, Colorado AIDS, Project Angel Heart, and The Gathering Place."

Faatma has a small crew of interns and a larger, more motley crew of volunteers. Brandy Gee weeds a row of greens. It's her first day and she's come to chill out and be in touch with the earth and to learn about community programs for her business idea, an urban general store. A young professional type, in hip flannel and designer jeans, is here because the court sent him to work off community hours. Then there's Hamadi.

Hamadi Mayange works at the farm most days. He rides the bus and he takes home a bag of vegetables after his day's work. Hamadi is fifty-nine, a Somali Bantu refugee. He grew food with his neighbors in his homeland, so he just likes being around the farm; it reminds him of home. When he leaves DeLaney, usually around two o'clock in the afternoon, he takes the bus back into the city, to his home neighborhood and the East Thirteenth Street Garden. Hamadi is the de facto leader of the Somali Bantu

A woman tends vegetables in the East Thirteenth Street Garden, once an empty lot.

community there. His two garden experiences—his African culture at East Thirteenth Street and the diverse American mix at DeLaney—span an interesting spectrum.

Back in the city, another DUG project, the Peace Garden, is tucked into a corner property surrounded by small homes on tight lots. Between 1992 and 1994, gang activity hit an intangible tipping point in Denver and murder became a rite of passage for many teenagers. Over one hundred young adults were killed in acts of violence. Anna Chavez's sixteen-year-old son, Troy, was one of them. Anna created The "Troy"

Chavez Foundation in the Sunny Side neighborhood to create hope and reduce gang violence.

She originally wanted to build a small corner garden as a memorial to her son. But then a narrow lot with burned-down greenhouses and weeds became available. The space had become a dangerous hangout for gangs, and Anna jumped at the chance to rehabilitate the lot into a clean, healthy part of the neighborhood, something to create positive change in light of her son's death and the violence pervading the city. In 1994, with the help of some neighbors and some heavy-duty, syringe-proof work gloves, she cleaned out the lot.

"We didn't have any money," Anna says. "We put a prayer here. We visioned it, as a community. Then things just started happening. DUG heard about us and offered skills and connections. We talked to young kids about their elders and their ancestors, the indigenous people of Mexico and Guatemala. Some of the kids who started the garden had buried their friends. They wanted a place to remember them, but also to feel safe and to find themselves."

So Anna and the kids designed the garden in the form of an Aztec ball court, with two ceremonial courtyards at the front surrounded by medicinal plantings of sage, yerba buena, St. John's wort, echinacea, comfrey, rosemary, and ceremonial tobacco. In the back half of the garden, a local alternative school manages crops alongside plots farmed by the community.

"We teach the kids about the old ways of our people," says Anna. "We descend from the natives of Mexico: Aztecs, Mayans, Toltecs, Chichimecas, Zapotecas. We've always been agricultural and connected to the land. This isn't new. We just want to bring it to the kids so we don't lose it.

"But I also tell the kids all the time, 'You belong here. You're not a foreigner. You have responsibilities here. That leads to pride and ownership and care for your place.'"

The Peace Garden has been working for sixteen years, but Anna still sees violence. A teenager named Jeremy was shot recently. His whole heart had been in the garden since his home life was a wreck. But Anna knows the garden brought peace to his life.

Each spring a big yellow butterfly returns to the Peace Garden. Anna believes it's the same one that arrived shortly after the garden began. When it first arrived, it landed on her finger and sat there for a moment, reconnecting to the place and to mom Chavez, a spiritual reminder of how her loss has been transformed into a positive gain for the community.

Many of the gardeners are refugees who cultivate the same vegetables they grew in their homelands.

ESTABLISHED: 1985.

SIZE: One hundred gardens totaling 24 acres.

MISSION: To create a thriving and connected network of deeply rooted community gardens in urban Denver, conceived of, cultivated, and supported by local residents and institutions.

WHO'S IN CHARGE: Board of directors (Chris Adams, president), executive director (Michael Buchenau), and twelve full-time staff who oversee eight interns.

SURROUNDING NEIGHBORHOOD: Metro Denver.

ZONING: Historic and residential.

FUNDING: Private foundations, corporations, City of Denver, City of Aurora, City of Golden, USDA, and Scientific and Cultural Facilities Districts of Denver and Arapahoe counties.

WHO EATS IT: Ninety-one CSA members at the DeLaney Farm, 246 WIC clients, and roughly 32,000 people involved in annual programming throughout all of the projects.

HOW TO   Turn Your Waste into Black Gold

Compost is nature's way of closing the ecological loop. In other words, it turns waste into food. Without this process, we'd be surrounded by piles of dead organic material. Instead, nature converts dead plants and animal waste into plant food through a chemical mineralization process we call composting. Farmers have been taking advantage of this for thousands of years to replenish nutrients in soils depleted from growing crops. Only recently has this age-old technique been abandoned, mainly because synthetic fertilizer offers a faster, easier, and, for now, cheaper way to replenish nutrients.

Unfortunately, two significant downsides accompany the use of synthetic fertilizer. The first is poor soil health. Synthetic fertilizers provide next year's crops with the basic nutrients for plants to grow, but they don't replenish the soil in the same way composting does. The result is a dramatic decrease in soil fertility wherever synthetic fertilizers are used, which is most of the world.

The second major drawback to the wholesale abandonment of composting in modern agriculture is a massive shift in how industrialized countries manage waste. Instead of fulfilling a clear demand for dead plant material and animal waste, most of these products are diverted to landfills and manure-holding ponds. Both approaches to waste management are expensive and can contribute to the spread of infectious diseases. America's food system uses about 60 percent of all the energy consumed in the country each year. This same food system fills municipal landfills with organic food waste as fast as any other single industry.

Fortunately, cities like San Francisco are beginning to develop ways to reduce waste. They have mandated that residents compost organic material instead of throwing it away. But even if cities and municipalities do not create policies or infrastructure to reduce waste, urban farms and individuals can do great things to help close the loop in their own cities and produce plenty of first-rate organic fertilizer at the same time.

Twenty years ago, Judy Elliot, education and community empowerment coordinator for Denver Urban Gardens, recognized that composting would be much more popular in Denver if residents knew the proper techniques and saw how easy it is to make fertilizer out of organic waste. Since Denver lacked a municipal composting operation, she helped start the Denver Urban Gardens Master Composting program to get more people involved. It's been a huge success. Judy provides an intensive training program to a core group of instructors who then go out into the community to teach others. The program includes training in basic biology and chemistry and field trips to local landfills and commercial compost facilities to see the impact of our waste-deposit choices.

DUG has developed a compost demonstration site to give residents a visual example of how easy composting can be. With this program, DUG is able to reach thousands of residents each year and keep tremendous amounts of valuable organic matter out of landfills. Judy also teaches Denver residents about the negative impact their lifestyle has on water quality and how they can minimize these effects.

Tips for Successful Composting

BUILD THE BIN. The cheapest and easiest compost bins are made of recycled pallets. Two pallets for the sides and one for the back create an instant bin. They just happen to come together into the perfect size: three feet by three feet by three feet. You can also use chicken wire and two-by-fours to make a quick and cheap bin.

ADD THE BROWN AND GREEN INGREDIENTS. Start with a six-inch layer of brown ingredients (see below) and then add a six-inch layer of green ingredients. Keep adding brown and green layers, alternating them, until all your ingredients are gone or the pile is four feet tall. Add water to each layer so that the final moisture level is the consistency of a wrung-out sponge.

TURN REGULARLY. Once the pile is built, the brown and green ingredients will chemically react and heat the pile up, known as "cooking" the ingredients. To ensure all the ingredients are cooking, use a pitchfork to turn the contents of the bin biweekly. Or, if you have purchased a rotating or tumbling bin, follow the manufacturer's directions. People often fail to turn smaller, covered bins. A three-by-three-foot open bin is ideal. Using a well-designed commercial bin, such as Bio-Stack, makes turning easier.

NURTURE. Composting is just like growing a garden. If you care for it and use the proper method and ingredients, the pile won't smell or attract rodents. The compost is ready for use when all the original ingredients are gone and the pile has cooled off.

Ingredients for Compost

Brown Stuff (Primary Source of Carbon)

LEAVES. Grab those bags of leaves from the side of the road and prevent nature's treasures from ending up in the landfill.
STRAW. Straw from cereal plants (barley, oats, wheat) works well, but avoid pine straw, as it is very acidic and slow to break down.
SAWDUST. Avoid wood from "treated lumber," which contains toxic chemicals.

Green Stuff (Primary Source of Nitrogen)

GRASS CLIPPINGS. Always ask if preemergent herbicide has been used on a lawn before taking clippings. Preemergent herbicide prevents fruit and vegetable seeds from germinating.
COFFEE GROUNDS. Despite being brown, these are the single best source for compost because they are filled with nitrogen and already finely ground.
KITCHEN SCRAPS. Eggshells and uncooked fruits and vegetables are ideal. Avoid meats, dairy products, and oils, which will attract rodents.
ANIMAL MANURE. Only get manure from animals that eat plants. The manure of carnivores can carry disease.

JUNIPER GARDENS AND CULTIVATE KANSAS CITY
KANSAS CITY, KANSAS AND MISSOURI

Seven women in ankle-length floral dresses bend at the waist in rows of kale, arugula, or kohlrabi. Their dark-chocolate hands effortlessly pull weeds and cut stems. The soft pink rising sun is already hot coming through the hazy white sky, making the distant Kansas City downtown look like a mirage. With the low-slung brick buildings of the Juniper Gardens public housing site on one side of the seven-acre farm, it's hard to know which is more out of place, more of an illusion: the city, the verdant farm, the parched yards of the apartments, or the farmer women from Burundi, Somalia, Myanmar (Burma), Bhutan, and Sudan.

Under a covered space between an office trailer and a walk-in refrigerator, a dozen more men and women, some of them young adults, wash and bundle the produce for Saturday's market. The vibrant colors of the vegetables and fruits, the fast pace of the washing and the moving of boxes, and the multiple languages being spoken could be a scene from a market in a dozen countries around the world. The setting is decidedly more authentic and real than the produce aisle of a typical grocery store.

The farm is called Juniper Gardens and the program for the women farmers is New Roots for Refugees. It is a joint project of the Catholic Charities of Northeast Kansas City and Cultivate Kansas City (CKC). The refugee women who work individual farm lots sell their produce at the city's network of farmer's markets, many of which have been created by CKC. The rest of Juniper Gardens has been given over to community plots for residents of the low-income and subsidized-housing neighborhood of northeast Kansas City, Kansas.

Kansas City straddles two states, Missouri and Kansas, and it is surrounded by the quintessential American heartland, the most agriculturally focused culture, political

Zawadi Daniel, a Burundi American, has been in the New Roots for Refugees farm training program since 2009.

scene, and economy in our country. Driving east through Kansas from Colorado reveals almost no evidence of actual food production, however. The state imports 97 percent of its produce. During the past one hundred years, fruit and vegetable farms have declined from 140,000 production acres to 7,700 acres. Fields of corn, soybeans, rice, cotton, and wheat extend to the horizons like a green sea broken by lighthouses of grain silos. And the small towns that punctuate the monocultures of commodity crops off Interstate 70—places like Evans, Russell, Bunker Hill—are approaching ghost-town status. They can't even support the icon of the rural American town, a mom-and-pop diner.

So, you must go into the core of the metropolis to see and understand the new ideas that might save farming in this state and be a model for the creation of the next step in the urban farm movement: development of an *industry* of sustainable food. That industry will embrace a healthy spectrum of food producers, ranging from large-scale peri-urban production farms (operations located at the edge of city and rural environments) to medium-sized urban parcels to vacant-lot city farms to neighbors selling one another tomatoes from their front yards.

Katherine Kelly is executive director and cofounder of CKC, and she's seen her neighbors begin selling tomatoes like kids selling curbside lemonade. Katherine believes in profitability; even such a tiny blip of urban agriculture as a front-yard tomato stand must turn a profit to create an industry of healthy food production that can survive over the long term.

Katherine grew up working on her neighbors' for-profit farms in Kansas. While living in Boston as an adult, she noticed a few nonprofit gardens in and around town. "Part of me felt that making the farm a nonprofit announces that it isn't viable," she says. "It acts like a museum and it's run like a museum sometimes. Farming shouldn't be like that. In a way, that says you've given up.

"I have to say there is a particularly midwestern emphasis on the free market as the solution. I don't like a lot of that—the idea that capitalism is the solution to everything. But I believe in small businesses, and I know and see how proud the owners are of their businesses."

At the Brookside Farmers' Market, in an upper-middle-class neighborhood of Kansas City, the CKC farm stand has the first tomatoes of the season. CKC grows on a prolific two acres in a suburban section of the city characterized by modest middle-income homes arranged in moderate density. Their for-profit farm sales have contributed over twenty-two thousand dollars to the organization over the last three years. CKC also supports, through services, expertise, and land-use access, farm projects like New Roots for Refugees.

Rachel Bonar was director of women's programs at Catholic Charities in 2005. The women in the Catholic Charities relief program are natives of Somalia, Sudan, Burundi, and Myanmar. All but one of them had grown up in agricultural communities that relied on small-scale farms for household sustenance. In their new home of Kansas City, the women had no access to land for planting. They began asking Rachel about the opportunity to grow food. So Rachel and some of the women started a community garden at the organization's office.

"Almost immediately we realized that these women are really good at growing food," says Rachel. "So the next year we partnered with CKC and began the New Roots farm."

The New Roots for Refugees farm is part community farm and part farm business program. The business program acts as an incubator farm for fourteen women. Once

A New Roots farmer looks out over the crops she'll eventually sell at a farmer's market.

The New Roots for Refugees farm includes seven acres behind the Juniper Gardens public housing site, where some of the refugee families live.

accepted into the program (and after at least one year with a community garden plot), the farmers receive a quarter-acre plot for their own small business. During the first year, everything—seeds, tools, water, marketing—is paid for. Rachel even sets up two CSA members for each plot. Gradually, the farmers take on more responsibility.

In the winter, the trainees take planning, production, and marketing courses and English instruction that focuses on farming and marketing needs. In their second and third years, they begin paying for things like seeds (purchased on-site from the seed store), marketing, and tools. They organize their own CSA member shares (between three and seven, normally). Rachel and the organization shuttle the farmers to and from the markets on the weekend, but the women are on their own selling the produce.

Six of the New Roots for Refugees farmers bring their produce to Brookside Farmers' Market, which has the trappings of a high-end Saturday farmer's market: grass-fed beef, artisanal cheeses, handmade yogurts, and booths overflowing with fresh, organic fruits and vegetables. The women who've recently arrived from Africa and Asia look elegant and proud in their vibrant dresses and evening shoes. Their produce is immaculate and sometimes exotic, native to their homelands but capable of cultivation here. Some of the refugee farmers have made up to three hundred dollars in a market day. Although not a large amount, it is a good supplement to their household incomes.

"I really have seen these women's disposition change," says Rachel. "They move to America from completely different worlds, and they often don't find anything they're good at. The language, the systems, the customs are all challenges. They aren't really eligible for other employment. Some go to the meat-processing plant to work, but it's so difficult there and worker laws so restrictive. Here they have the ownership. The work is all about self-determination, so they get out what they put in.

"Everyone needs something to be good at, and these women have found it. They're proud to provide ethnic food to their community. Some weekends Dena Tu, a Karen from Myanmar, drives hours to Omaha to bring ethnic vegetables to the Karen population up there."

The goal of the Farm Business Development Program is that after three years, the farmers, who have been saving two hundred dollars of their annual sales, will be able to start their own independent farm on a vacant lot within the neighborhood. Although it is a long shot that the farms will generate enough income for the farmers

A Bhutanese refugee checks her plot prior to market day.

to single-handedly support their families—most have husbands with full-time work—they do provide an invaluable monetary supplement, as well as putting healthy food on the farmers' tables and satisfying the essential human hunger for productivity and worthiness.

To Katherine Kelly, at CKC, the development of new farmers like the refugee women fits into the larger picture of the urban farm movement and even the overall national and global progression toward a more vibrant, sustainable food system. CKC also supports people like Sherri Harvel, an independent "rogue" city farmer.

Sherri works a vacant lot in southeast Kansas City, Missouri. Growing up, she spent a lot of time in the neighborhood visiting her grandmother. She holds a part-time job at Target, amounting to roughly twenty-five hours a week in the summer, when she spends much of her time tending the small farm. Sherri sells her produce at city farmer's markets and through a CSA of around ten members. One year she made ten thousand dollars in a single growing season from produce sales, though she values the emotional and physical benefits of the small farm, what she calls her sanctuary, as much as the profits.

Kansas is basically one state-sized farm, and it's hard to miss the irony at play in the state. America's breadbasket can't grow its own fruit and vegetables on some of the most fertile land in the world, land subsidized by one of the world's largest economies, yet a few independent growers working the poor city soils and supported by a nonprofit umbrella organization stand at the forefront of the state's and the country's new agricultural revolution.

"I look at what we do," says Katherine, "and to me, a healthy industry has small-small, small, medium, medium-large, and large forms. All of them are seeking to make profit and provide jobs. And the overall industry also includes nonprofits that provide social services and education. We need a lot of players at every level. It's ironic to hear these industrial and capitalist words come out of my mouth, but I really believe agriculture needs to be something people make a living from in order for it to be taken seriously."

Katherine is taking a giant evolutionary step in the urban farm movement. And yet it's not idealism that sits around the corner in this movement's progression forward. Rather, it's stone-cold practicality, the American way of supplying a demand and making a profit by selling valuable goods to consumers. It's a big-picture approach with its hands in the Kansas City soil. On the whole, Katherine believes that a new food *industry* must be created.

"We need home gardeners, community gardeners, commercial gardeners. When you've got that mix, you've got resilience and sustainability. You've got knowledge that passes along and a support infrastructure with the necessary tools, supplies, and services. Then you've got an industry, a really healthy community of industry.

"In Kansas and in general, we're land abundant and farmer poor," she says. "I've had so many people call me with one hundred acres and no one to farm it. People live in cities, so at some level we have to deal with that."

Turning our gaze into America's cities, then, proves to be one of the best ways to decipher the next steps in the food revolution, which are basically concepts and solutions that can be employed on a small scale within a dense environment. But Kansas City represents a crucial opportunity for expansion. The ideas and entrepreneurial spirit of the young farmers, immigrants, and part-time vacant-lot growers in Kansas

City must move out of the heartland's big city and into the heartland itself. In Kansas City, perhaps more than any other city, the urban farm movement's possibilities for systemic change are inching closer to expanding into America's breadbasket.

ESTABLISHED: 2004.

SIZE: 2 acres at the CKC farm, 7 acres at Juniper Gardens.

MISSION: To promote the production and consumption of fresh, local produce by urban farmers who are active members of healthy neighborhoods in greater Kansas City.

WHO'S IN CHARGE: Board of directors, executive director (Katherine Kelly), associate director (Dan Dermitzel), and three staff.

SURROUNDING NEIGHBORHOOD: New Roots for Refugees is in a low-income neighborhood and adjacent to a subsidized housing project. The CKC farm is in a middle-income neighborhood with mid-density single-family homes.

ZONING: Residential.

FUNDING: Foundation grants, corporate and individual donations, produce sales, contracted services.

WHO EATS IT: CSA members and farmer's market buyers that include food-stamp holders who receive dollar-for-dollar matching grants from local foundations.

HOW TO   Access Start-Up Capital for Urban Food Projects

Inner-city kids putting seeds in the ground and munching on deep green leaves of kale, vacant lots transformed into flower-filled hubs of community activity, food banks receiving thousands of pounds of fresh, local produce—the social and environmental benefits of urban farming are easy to see. The economic benefits, however, are much harder to understand.

Creating a viable business is the essential next step for urban farming to expand and become a more pervasive part of our food system. In order to be sustainable, urban and peri-urban farms must move away from being viewed as charities and into a decidedly free-market realm that attracts the best and the brightest business minds. Innovative business techniques are just as important in developing what Katherine Kelly calls the new *industry* of healthy food as innovative growing techniques are.

One example of a proven, simple, and replicable business model is SPIN (small plot intensive farming). It provides a framework for new urban farmers to see how the properly scaled farm can be profitable and fit into the built environment. On a small urban lot, or even on a collection of backyards, and with minimal equipment investment, a novice grower can make a legitimate income. For instance, SPIN projects, which don't require land ownership (plots are rented, borrowed, or bartered), have been proven to gross fifty thousand dollars on a half acre. Roxanne Christensen of SPIN points out that because most urban farmers are not professionals, the movement is at risk of being perceived as not commercially viable by city planners, developers, or potential investors. Calling the movement sub-acre commercial agriculture gives the enterprise legitimacy and makes it compatible with urban development. (For more information on SPIN, see www.spinfarming.com.)

Sustainable agriculture is no different from any other industry: there can be no single tried-and-true business model. The scale of an operation is the most crucial question. You have to decide what scale you want to farm at and match that to your market.

As urban farming continues to grow in diverse ways, it will conform to its social, natural, economic, and political environments. There will always be room for long-term nonprofit urban farms, just as there is room for nonprofits in other industries. But a conscious effort is being made to illuminate and champion business practices that generate profit and will therefore encourage more urban farms, farmers, and good food.

Tips for Accessing Start-Up Capital

For more urban farms to become profitable, they need access to capital. But the traditional methods for financing farming operations are not available to most urban farmers. Because few urban farmers own their land, they can't leverage it for start-up capital. Even if they could, the small-scale nature of these operations doesn't make it feasible. Additionally, most urban farmers aren't confident enough in their skills to risk going into debt to get a project started.

As with so many businesses, the real hurdle for getting an urban food project off the ground is often start-up capital. Here's some advice on overcoming that hurdle.

START SMALL. Jones Valley Urban Farm (page 91) started small—really small. JVUF's first urban farm plot was less than a quarter acre. Since then it has been easier to grow bigger than it is to shrink: success builds on success.

SCALE UP. CKC has developed an apprenticeship program that gives new growers everything they need to get started and assistance with marketing their products. They have adapted a matched-savings program that requires new growers to contribute their earnings to a pool of money for the first two years of operation. After they have completed the program, CKC matches the money they have saved. This allows growers to "scale up" and use their skills to become profitable.

PARTNER WITH A DEVELOPER. Prairie Crossing (page 153) instituted a transaction fee: every home in the new community pays a small fee to support the start-up costs of the farm. Now Sandhill Organics is a for-profit operation and benefits everyone. Many new developers are incorporating urban farms into their designs.

PARTNER WITH A CITY AND/OR NONPROFIT. The City of Montgomery, Alabama, allocated two and a half acres of open space along the riverfront for an urban farm. A partnership with a local nonprofit institute makes management of the farm simple and a win-win situation for everyone. Every city in America has land it has to pay to maintain. The key is making the city understand how it could cost *less* to create a farm than to mow the grass.

APPLY FOR GRANTS. The U.S. Department of Agriculture has numerous sources of funding to help start or scale up new farming enterprises. While the applications can be challenging, the programs are waiting for you to apply. Check out the USDA's Community Food Program for more information.

VERSAILLES COMMUNITY
NEW ORLEANS, LOUISIANA

East New Orleans is lush and crumbling. Sometimes it feels like the built environment—the convenience stores, the sugar factories, the distant oil refineries, the houses, the brick apartments, the parking-lot pavement—is no different from the vegetation, all bloom and decay, the life cycle spinning in time-lapse. Strip malls cling like painter's tape to the side of Chef Menteur Highway, and between the asphalt and behind it, the wetland jungle seems to be breathing its hot, wet air onto everything.

This eastern stretch of the Big Easy lies between Lake Pontchartrain and Lake Borgne, a lagoon inlet of the Gulf of Mexico. About ten miles east, Chef Menteur (aka Highway 90) continues for almost forty miles across the Rigolets (pronounced *RIG-o-lees*), a wild and undeveloped strait of pine forests and swamp.

But before it disappears into that swamp, Highway 90 passes Versailles, a neighborhood of vinyl-sided or light-colored brick ranch houses in a perfectly midcentury suburban layout with sidewalks, a few main boulevards—Dwyer, Michoud, and Alcee Fortier—and a couple shopping centers at the highway's edge. On the north side of town, a low mound covered in tangled weeds and shrubs marks the levee that holds in the Pontchartrain overflow. Beyond that lie Lake Michoud, the larger Blind Lagoon, and a soggy swamp in between.

Six thousand Vietnamese Americans live in this American village. The market at Alcee Fortier's shopping center could be transplanted straight from Ho Chi Minh City. Most of the items don't exist in mainstream American supermarkets. Fresh produce—mainly greens—sits in boxes scattered about the space. A steady buzz pervades the store, the type of movement and noise that seems both chaotic and comfortable.

Father Luke Nguyen visits the thriving garden of one of his parishioners.

A large wave of Vietnamese refugees arrived in New Orleans in the mid-1970s. Following the Vietnam War, many southern Vietnamese were deemed enemies by the reunified communist state. Because the United States government felt a responsibility to protect the people who had fought alongside American soldiers, they allowed thousands of Vietnamese to immigrate and settled them in a handful of American locations with relief services and adequate housing to absorb them. New Orleans fit the profile. It had a strong Catholic Charities presence (many of the refugees were Catholic) and its Versailles neighborhood had a glut of mostly abandoned but functional housing. In addition, the local neotropical Mississippi Delta climate shares many of the hot, humid, and rainy characteristics of the Mekong Delta.

The Vietnamese settled into the relatively uninhabited new developments of East New Orleans. They became Gulf fishermen or they worked in factories, hotels, and restaurants throughout New Orleans. In little square suburban backyards, the new immigrants grew vegetables and fruits from seeds brought over from Vietnam. Some even crossed the levee and planted in the fertile, undevelopable land on the other side. The wet fields, delta soils, and thick, heavy air accommodated the same plants that grew in Vietnam, and everyone, especially the elderly, knew how to grow things— that's what they did back home.

My Tran is in her thirties and a Versailles resident. She grew up here and her parents still live in a modest ranch house with a vibrant backyard that overflows with rows of greens all the way to the canal side. She works with the Mary Queen of Vietnam Church, the strongest institution in a community that is 90 percent Catholic and 10 percent Buddhist. Most members of the older generation attend mass every morning at 6:30 a.m.

My's parents arrived in America in 1975. They farm a plot in the commonly shared community space along a black-water canal. At work in their conical straw hats, with banana trees silhouetted against the hazy blue sky, water lilies choking the still canal, and a hundred shades of green surrounding them, they could be at the center of an iconic scene on a Vietnamese postcard. But their stories of hard work and scrappiness are at the heart of the American dream.

"When we were younger," says My, "my parents grew vegetables for home and for sale at market. They made over half of their income from the market sales. They came here with no education, no language. Dad was a plumber and mom cut grass for minimum wage. They tended the garden at nights and on weekends. All nine of

their kids went to college. My grandfather did the original farming—he passed it on to my parents."

Hurricane Katrina hit the residents of Versailles hard. A commitment to return to their homes following the flood and a rock-solid work ethic laid the foundation for recovery. But it was the skills and the history of growing their own food in community spaces and backyards that helped make that recovery quick and successful. A lot of motivation for what we're calling food security comes from a fear of natural disasters such as Katrina. What happens when the transportation avenues we've come to rely on for our trucked-in food get damaged? Much of the Versailles community's rapid recovery can be traced to their food security. Their ability to feed themselves independent of the larger national food system network laid the groundwork for the more intricate recovery efforts, like founding a charter school to replace the closed-down public school.

Food security was not a last-minute effort following Katrina. By that time, it was too late to develop the food-growing capacity to respond to such devastation. Since the

The majority of growers in Versailles are local retirees who raise food for their home, for their children and grandchildren, and to sell at a local market.

81

The flood zones along the canals of East New Orleans's Versailles neighborhood are perfect for growing traditional Vietnamese crops.

1970s, the food economy of Versailles has been largely a local one. Backyards produce enough for the family and for excess sales to the local Vietnamese restaurants and food markets. Without stringent regulations or organic certifications, the Saturday open-air farmer's market welcomes all comers. It looks and operates like a marketplace in Vietnam.

The Catholic Church wants to take advantage of that market mentality and the retired residents' interest in growing food for sale. The idea for an organized, designed urban farm and market in the neighborhood began with the charismatic Father Vien, of Mary Queen of Vietnam Church. Early in the 2000s, he recognized the community advantages of having the farm and market. It would provide an organized space where growers could gather and a forum for education and instruction to younger generations of farmers and gardeners. It would also draw outside visitors, thus expanding the potential for farmers to make money selling their produce. The basic sketch, then, went into a charette held by the City Center, a design-build outreach program at Tulane University, and Spackman Mossop Michaels, a New Orleans landscape architecture firm. The model has evolved to its final stage and has received national acclaim with an exhibit in New York's Cooper-Hewitt Museum.

The project is called the Viet Village Urban Farm and will fill in twenty-eight acres of wetland. For years, residents had rogue farms scattered throughout the wetland that sits on the other side of a levee. But since Katrina, the canals and low-lying areas have been flooded, all but ruining the wetland plots. The Viet Village project, however, will create a consolidated space for the farming that has been going on in the community for over thirty years. The six-million-dollar Viet Village will include community plots, quarter-acre market farm plots for commercial growing, a storm-water reservoir, and a composting facility. It will incorporate a covered market space for produce sales and a livestock grazing area, plus a small meat-processing plant for immediate, direct meat production and sales. It's an ambitious idea that would put a shiny American design onto the old-world institution of growing food to sell and eat.

But it also raises questions. The Vietnamese immigrants have been operating in an unregulated environment for the past three decades. The men and women who grow produce or harvest shrimp and seafood bring the products to the corner shopping centers for the Saturday market in a style still practiced in Vietnam and other countries where regulations are lax or nonexistent. They sell their shrimp and catfish fillets from coolers and produce from boxes that sit on the ground. Farmer's markets

in America are subject to U.S. Department of Agriculture regulations and inspections, and government authorities occasionally arrive in Versailles and shut down vendors selling catfish or shrimp or produce. Some community men and women no longer sell their goods at the market out of fear.

Landscape architect Wes Michaels trusts that the Versailles farmers will adapt to the Louisiana food regulations that have been largely demystified over the years because of the proliferation of street vendors and food festivals throughout New Orleans and Louisiana. "We've had meetings with the state's agriculture regulators about the Vietnamese farmers processing meat in their traditional way. The guys from the agriculture department seem pretty open to the traditional market style of the Vietnamese," says Michaels.

Currently, the Viet Village is in a holding pattern. Since it will be developed on wetlands, the project must undergo the U.S. Corps of Engineers' environmental assessment process. But first, a permit must be obtained through the mitigation bank, a third-party stewardship agreement managed by, in this case, Chevron. The mitigation bank stipulates that its owner, Chevron, must enhance the environmental quality

Trung Tran harvests greens growing along her backyard fence.

85

of the property in perpetuity. So, if something goes wrong, such as contamination, habitat loss, or the like, Chevron, not the Viet Village farm, is responsible.

The cost of the permit is $380,000. The Mary Queen of Vietnam Community Development Corporation (CDC) has reached out to Chevron to transfer mitigation bank credits for the property, but the timeline for transferring credits runs up to five years. So in order to keep the project moving forward, the CDC is looking to raise the money necessary to buy the permit straight up, rather than be subjected to the legal process of credit transfer from Chevron. The Viet Village's proposed site is on sensitive, federally managed land, and it's a big enough project that the Corps of Engineers must go by the books in following proper land-use practices and protocol. With the well-planned, official farm market and village comes the obstacle of official regulation, a double-edged sword for many urban farm operations that operate under the radar of city ordinances. A lack of regulation means less hassle on the farmer's end, but a stamp of certified approval could attract those customers who are skeptical of purchasing food from an "unofficial" market.

The Viet Village Urban Farm would simply put a formal exclamation point on this community's thriving food-production example. Walking through backyards overflowing with greens, potatoes, and fruits, and then eating the produce at the nearby *phở* restaurant and seeing backyard vegetables sold at the market on Alcee Fortier leaves the impression that Versailles is a model for sustainable local food, even though no one calls it that. It's just what they do: there's soil and there's sun and there's water. Why wouldn't you grow food there?

Father Luke Nguyen, an assistant to Father Vien, wonders if the propensity to garden will survive the current elder generation. Are flat screens and fast food, the pastimes of too many youths, going to bulldoze the native knowledge and tourniquet the green thumbs? And will state agriculture regulations inhibit the free-market commerce of the community's current food system, thus scaring away potential backyard market farmers? He doesn't see it that way. Father Luke, like Father Vien, says it's a tradition that makes too much sense to pass away.

"It's not just *this* elderly generation who wants to farm and enjoys being outside gardening and raising food," says Father Luke. "It's just the elders. Period. There will always be elders. Other retirees pass the time playing bridge, tennis, golf, or volunteering at parks and the like. In the Vietnamese community, the elderly and retired stay busy growing food."

This turns many contemporary notions of continuity and sustainability on their head. In Versailles, the young people are encouraged to go on to be professionals and work and raise their families. When they have retired, they can dig in, connect with their heritage, and grow food in the backyard of the American Dream.

ESTABLISHED: 1975.

SIZE: Plots range from 20 square feet in backyards to ¼ acre on the canal banks. The Viet Village Urban Farm is planned for 28 acres.

MISSION: The goal of the Viet Village Urban Farm is to improve local food system sustainability and security while increasing economic opportunities for community members and providing a culturally rich community space.

WHO'S IN CHARGE: Individuals manage their own plots and sell as independent vendors at the market and to the restaurants. The Mary Queen of Vietnam Community Development Corporation directs the Viet Village Urban Farm project.

SURROUNDING NEIGHBORHOOD: Predominantly lower- to middle-class Vietnamese Americans and African Americans.

ZONING: Residential (backyards) and canal banks.

FUNDING: The Catholic Church provides some local support, but most of the gardens are funded by the individuals who work them. The Viet Village Urban Farm is funded by the EPA Brownfields Program, Market Umbrella, Robert Wood Johnson Foundation, Ford Foundation, New Orleans Food and Farm Network, Tulane City Center (in-kind), Te-Enterprise (in-kind), and Spackman Mossop Michaels (in-kind). As of 2010, funding for the $380,000 permit for wetlands mitigation and for the $1.5 million phase I construction is being sought.

WHO EATS IT: The households growing the food and the Versailles community via market sales and restaurants.

HOW TO Develop a Congregational Urban Farm

Father Luke Nguyen knows everyone growing food in Versailles. The entire neighborhood is like his parish, his minidiocese. He walks into backyard gardens and onto canal-bank plots like he walks down the aisle of Mary Queen of Vietnam Church. The social-religious mix comes so naturally because the Vietnamese community of East New Orleans has been interwoven with the Catholic Church since before the refugees left their homeland following the Vietnam War. The Catholic Church's strong New Orleans presence and availability of social services made the city a viable relocation option. So, on almost every initiative and activity, the church and the community act as one.

It's a seemingly unique relationship, but, when you look closely at faith-based centers—synagogues, temples, churches—in cities and small towns throughout the country, the interconnections between community building projects and faith-based centers become clear. And there's great potential on that hyperlocal level for what some call *congregational gardening*. It's the same idea as community gardening, only within the realm of a specific congregation with a shared faith and mission, rather than a shared geographic neighborhood.

In Eugene, Oregon, the Lane County Food Bank (FOOD) operates a two-and-a-half-acre farm on the property of the St. Thomas Episcopal Church. The partnership between church and food bank affords space for Lane County Master Gardeners, youth groups, schools, and community members to collaborate in maintaining the property. Each year, around ninety thousand pounds of produce are distributed by FOOD to low-income families. In this case, a church is offering land while not being involved in the maintenance of the farm.

It's generally rare for a church not to have a lawn on its property, and not to have some members of its congregation interested in giving back to the community. So instead of paying someone to mow the grass, many churches are tilling the earth and planting seeds. While these intentions can be noble, it's important to ensure that the sweat is rewarded. Here are some things to consider before digging in.

Planning a Congregational Garden

FIND A NEED. Are there individuals or groups who can use the produce you will grow? For example, fresh produce is harder for seniors or single mothers to use than canned or frozen food. It also requires refrigeration, something not everyone has access to all of the time. Make sure your produce has a home before you start growing it.

DECIDE WHAT TO PLANT. Interview local food banks about what kinds of food are in demand before putting seeds in the ground. While lettuce may seem like a great thing to grow, sweet potatoes or tomatoes may be what are needed.

EXTEND THE SHELF LIFE. Is there a way to process the fresh produce into canned goods or preserves? The opportunities for use increase significantly when storage time is not as limited.

MANAGE THE GARDEN. Producing usable amounts of food requires a lot more work than just breaking up the soil and planting seeds. Effective food gardens need to be weeded, watered, and replanted regularly to ensure the yields are maximized. It's important to match the size of the garden with the available labor, either volunteer or paid.

FIND A PARTNER. Is there a food bank that can pick up the garden produce on a regular basis? Many communities already have trucks picking up donated food or recovering excess food. Adding the church garden to existing routes is a good way to ensure quick distribution and increase the garden's effectiveness.

MAKE IT SOCIAL. Church and other institution-based gardens can be particularly effective at tapping into members' desire to have a positive impact in their community beyond donating money. Arranging work parties after church services can tap into that sentiment and give members a chance to put their faith into action.

Summers in Birmingham almost hum with heat. The stifling air shimmers off the pavement of downtown and few people venture outdoors. Those who do, try not to move much. But on the block between Twenty-fifth Street North and Seventh Avenue North, a group of foodies gathers basil and red peppers. They planted the seedlings months ago, and they'll take the harvest directly to the kitchen to prepare a fresh pesto for homemade pizza. But their kitchen is not at one of the restaurants of Birmingham's James Beard Award winner Frank Stitt or at the equally prestigious establishment of Chris Hastings. Rather, the foodies at Jones Valley Urban Farm (JVUF) are eleven- to fifteen-year-olds participating in a week-long summer Foodie Camp. Their kitchen is in the YMCA Youth Center a block from the farm. Many of them have never pulled edibles from the ground or tasted pesto.

Edwin Marty left his role as an experiential educator in sailing and mountaineering with Washington State's Pacific Crest Outward Bound School to bring urban farming to his hometown of Birmingham. But he did not leave behind the educational ethos gained in a decade of teaching. From the beginning, Marty intended the urban farm project, which he started on a single abandoned lot in Birmingham's Southside neighborhood, to be an educational tool. Birmingham needed fresh ideas in education as much as it needed fresh, local food. The health of Birmingham's largely lower-income city population was plummeting, reflecting the health dilemma facing the entire state. In a 2005 study conducted by a statewide committee for the Alabama State Board of Education, Alabama ranked in the top three states in the nation in rates of excessive weight, diabetes, and hypertension among adults. And the children fared no better than the adults. According to the Jefferson County Department of Health,

Edwin Marty tends to the seedlings that are ready to be planted out in the fields. They are a combination of vegetables, fruits, herbs, and flowers for cutting.

of which Birmingham is the major part, the percentage of overweight third graders increased from 12.8 percent in 2002–2003 to 22.1 percent in 2008–2009.

Jones Valley Urban Farm took advantage of those numbers to gain traction in funding for an educational farm and nutrition programs. Just by way of geographic proximity to a dense population, any urban farm intrinsically offers a modicum of education and outreach to the public regarding healthy food and healthy lifestyles. People see an urban farm. Even if they don't engage with it or eat the food, the simple act of riding a bike down a sidewalk and seeing chickens pecking the soil behind a fence or watching the rows of beans grow taller among their trellises as the summer progresses creates a level of exposure and awareness that doesn't exist for many urban dwellers who have never been outside the city limits. But with some effort, the urban farm presents an abundant array of educational opportunities—teachable moments—that can fill gaps left vacant by underfunded schools.

Even before Marty expanded his Southside farm onto the much larger Park Place lot in downtown Birmingham in 2007, he prioritized education. He hired Rachel Reinhart as education director in 2006. Rachel had been working as an experiential educator since 1987. Experiential education involves hands-on, kinesthetic teaching and learning methodology. All students learn in a handful of ways, including reading, writing, speaking, acting, and actually *doing*. Traditional classrooms are limited in their ability to explore a wide variety of teaching styles and usually end up concentrating primarily on book learning and memorization, especially with the current emphasis on standardized testing to rate school and faculty performance. But the outdoor classroom, whether it be in the forest, on a river, or at a farm, can offer many more learning avenues for reaching students.

Rachel now oversees a dozen educational programs at JVUF, from half-day elementary-school field trips to the farm and the week-long Foodie Summer Camp to a year-long, accredited agriscience course at the Alabama School of Fine Arts (ASFA), a public magnet school. JVUF currently has three full-time program staff and has expanded to include weekend workshops for adults interested in growing food, cooking, or starting their own community gardens. Considering that the Alabama state standards for teaching nutrition basically begin and end at the federal government's food pyramid—aka MyPyramid—bringing city and suburban students to a working production farm catapults the students' breadth of food and nutrition knowledge to a level impossible to achieve without a farm like Jones Valley.

Young farmers learn to operate a plow at JVUF's satellite farm in the planned community of Mt. Laurel.

"The MyPyramid tells how many servings per day kids are supposed to have," Rachel says. "They might learn the info, but they aren't putting it into practice. On the farm, we are able to see in real life what the foods are and how to make practical choices about food. And, maybe most importantly, we can show them how to make foods taste good."

Numerous studies have shown that if children or young adults try a new food item three times, they are very likely to incorporate the new item into their diet on a regular basis. The idea that kids just intrinsically don't like vegetables may simply be because they have never seen broccoli or kale or red peppers. Instead of instructing students about vegetables by showing them a cartoonlike pyramid, the farm allows them to experience food nutrition. When they walk up to a garden row, grab a green top, and pull a carrot from the ground, it's as magical as Harry Potter. That live, hands-on experience sparks the student's innate proclivity toward curiosity and experimentation.

"I've had parents come out to the farm and ask how we got their kid to want to eat broccoli—to actually *ask* for it at dinner," Rachel says. "We just showed it to them and had them pick it, then we cooked it together."

Jones Valley Urban Farm is located on a vacant city block adjacent to a mixed-income public housing development.

Rachel's agriscience course at the ASFA goes a step beyond the summer camp and field trip programs. The course counts for a lab credit within the state science curriculum, and students must complete one lab for each year of high school, four total to graduate. The students who finish the class successfully can apply for summer employment on the farm, a twenty-hour-per-week job that pays eight dollars an hour for the first summer. Part of the student interns' summer workload involves developing and carrying out a research project on some aspect of the farm. The research must be something that JVUF can actually use. For example, one student researched what insect pests were plaguing the farm and then came up with ways to deal with them organically. Thus, the ASFA agriscience course and summer intern program are symbiotic. The students follow their passion for agriculture and food-systems science without having to leave the city, and JVUF receives motivated, trained seasonal employees and research.

The education side of JVUF hits on all cylinders. It provides "between the bells" state-accredited course work during school hours, and "after the bells" programming for kids who need structure between the end of the school day and returning home.

JVUF is not an Edible Schoolyard, the food and nutrition program begun in Berkeley, California, by Alice Waters and adopted by dozens of schools around the country. The Edible Schoolyard is more a garden (and accompanying curriculum) within a school. Jones Valley, on the other hand, is a working production farm that teaches. That's an important distinction. JVUF's mission includes teaching youth and adults about healthy eating, and the farm's programs dive into sensitive, challenging, community- and statewide arenas, such as instructing school cafeteria employees on preparing fresh foods and working on rewriting city and state policy to facilitate a school cafeteria's incorporation of fresh, local fruits and vegetables over canned and processed options.

But first and foremost, JVUF's core farm at Park Place needs to produce goods to be sold. The challenge of instruction versus production arises at JVUF, repeating the dilemma of other instructional and job-training urban farms, like Santa Cruz's Homeless Garden Project (page 25) and Chicago's Growing Home farm (page 141). JVUF relies on its produce and flower sales to fund its operation and, partly, its educational programming. The older ASFA summer student farm employees and volunteer interns from the University of Alabama at Birmingham contribute greatly to the farm's output and thus its income. But it became clear that allowing younger students to harvest and sow inhibited production. The remedy was the creation of a separate children's garden.

Farm manager Katie Davis grows and sells flowers at local farmer's markets and grocery stores. Cut flowers are profitable, attact beneficial insects, and can instantly beautify a vacant lot.

JVUF offers small raised beds to both immediate neighbors and other residents throughout Birmingham. For first-time growers, JVUF provides classes on basic organic farming techniques.

Marty and staff secured funding to develop a small plot of stone wall–lined raised beds at the front of the farm, near the existing cluster of community raised beds. Students participated in the planning, and the new site offers a chance for learning that does not tax production on the working farm. It's the kind of innovation and adaptation that highlights the urban farm's pivotal role in supplementing the education systems in American cities, a vital battleground against obesity and nutrition-related diseases like hypertension and diabetes.

Marty and company recognized from its inception that the farm, with all its moving parts and its easy connection to the dinner table, offered an obvious expansion to the school classroom. It brings an entire living world into the city, and, once keen networking skills have brought in the student audience, the rows of carrots and strawberries and broccoli can become an ideal interdisciplinary classroom.

ESTABLISHED: 2002.

SIZE: 3½ acres at Park Place and 25 acres at suburban Mt. Laurel.

MISSION: To help Birmingham grow organic produce and healthy communities through urban farming and education.

WHO'S IN CHARGE: Executive director supervised by a twenty-member board of directors.

SURROUNDING NEIGHBORHOOD: JVUF's main farm and campus, known as Park Place, was created on an abandoned lot in downtown Birmingham. A mixed-income Hope VI community, an affordable housing project of the federal Housing and Urban Development program, surrounds the farm.

ZONING: Commercial.

FUNDING: 25 percent earned income (produce sales and education programs), 25 percent private donations and events, and 50 percent public and private grants.

WHO EATS IT: Fifty-member CSA, a pair of upscale farmer's markets, upscale restaurants, and farm stands at both the urban and suburban farms.

HOW TO   Engage the Community with Education Programs

There is little doubt that an urban garden project can have a positive impact on a community. Beautifying a vacant lot or increasing access to fresh, healthy food is a straightforward outcome that everyone can see. There is an assumption, however, that building an urban farm, community garden, or school garden will inherently yield these positive outcomes as well as other, more altruistic results, such as community empowerment. This assumption of inherent goodness has unfortunately prevented many well-intentioned projects from realistically matching the available resources with the changes originally envisioned by the organizers. The inherent-goodness attitude can also lead to a lack of accountability for a project's outcomes and can, subsequently, be a challenge to an urban farm's long-term sustainability within a community.

Projects that have instead viewed themselves as facilitators and collaborators with a community—by listening to the concerns of the community and by cultivating leadership within the community—tend to have a more profound impact that lasts over time. In *City Bountiful,* a history of community gardening in the United States, Laura Lawson points to the "importance of articulating the objective of an urban garden program in terms that can be validated."

Building a garden won't necessarily decrease a neighborhood's crime rate or increase the health indicators. But with intention and good collaborations that are logically evaluated, the garden can be the first step toward real, positive impacts in the farm's immediate area.

The most obvious way for an urban food project to achieve this goal is to partner with existing community organizations, often educational institutions, and to provide opportunities that would not exist without the garden. It's really all about building good relationships.

Making Partnership Work

Jones Valley Urban Farm collaborates with community groups, academic institutions, and faith-based groups to increase their educational impacts. Here are some examples.

Primary and Secondary Schools

EXPLORE COMMON INTERESTS. JVUF partnered with a local fine-arts high school that was looking for a way to get their students out of their inner-city school building and into the community. The school's foundation provided expertise at grant writing, and a pilot summer project received funding through the U.S. Department of Agriculture. From there, it turned into an accredited academic course that provides the farm with skilled interns.

After-School Programs

FIND LOCAL RESOURCES. JVUF joined forces with the YMCA Youth Center down the street from the farm to develop the Seed 2 Plate field trip. The after-school students at the YMCA come to the farm once a week to participate in the gardening component of the program. Then the JVUF instructor and the students walk back to the YMCA to use the teaching kitchen for the cooking and nutrition components. This seven-year collaboration has enabled JVUF to provide programs for a wide spectrum of students that go well beyond the original vision.

Exchange Program with Rural Community

STRENGTHEN NATURAL ALLIANCES. JVUF and a youth-leadership program in the Black Belt of Alabama have developed an exchange program that allows JVUF students to visit rural farms and rural students to visit the urban farm. Through this exchange, the urban high-school students come to better understand the challenges rural farm communities face, and the rural high-school students come to better understand the market potentials in a city and how an urban farm can cultivate that market.

Colleges and Universities

RECRUIT LOCAL STUDENTS. Many colleges and universities have programs that will pay their students to work on community projects, such as urban farms. Jones Valley Urban Farm has programs with multiple local colleges where students gain exposure to a small-business operation and learn growing techniques, and the farm gets free labor and an energized community.

County Health Departments

SHARE THE MESSAGE. Urban farms can act as potent "vehicles" for many local health departments seeking alternative means of delivering their health messages. JVUF teamed up with the county health department to develop a school cafeteria training program called Delicious/Nutritious that teaches cafeteria staffs simple ways to provide more healthful food to their students, focusing on local, fresh ingredients.

GREENSGROW FARMS AND THE PHILADELPHIA PROJECT
PHILADELPHIA, PENNSYLVANIA

It's sunny and 94° F and the pavement steams after a thunderstorm rolled sideways through north Philly. Mary Seton Corboy wears a full-body white bee suit. She stands on the grassy roof of a small shed on a vacant city lot. Smoke puffs from the antique-looking box in her hand and the bees calm down. "We put these up here originally just for security," she says. "Figured no one would bother the equipment with a bunch of bees around."

On one city block Corboy has created a small world with a split personality of sorts. There is Greensgrow, the farm, CSA, and nursery business, and there's The Philadelphia Project, a 501c.3 parent organization that oversees all the operations. So this small world is diverse and open to new ideas. The shed under the beehives holds farm tools. Beside the shed, tanks for the biodiesel-conversion operation transform used cooking oil into fuel for Big Yellow, the delivery truck that collects fresh produce and meat and dairy products from farms within seventy-five miles of Greensgrow's square of green in Philadelphia's Kensington neighborhood. The farm-direct food is sold at local farmer's markets and distributed among four hundred CSA members. The nursery sells plants and starter vegetables.

These three income sources—the farm-direct sales, the CSA, and the nursery— earn close to one million dollars a year. It's a viable business that can support itself. After paying staff and maintenance out of the revenue, the remaining profit ($70,000 in 2010) goes into the other side of Greensgrow's split personality, the overarching nonprofit, The Philadelphia Project. This side allows for the in-kind donations and corporate support that amount to 15 percent of the organization's budget and, as Corboy says, "keeps us on the up and up."

Although the Greensgrow site, a former steel plant and Brownfields zone, was long ago remediated by the EPA, raised beds are used for everything from nursery plants to kale.

Greensgrow's hybrid nature renders it nearly solvent financially (85 percent of its budget is generated by the farm and nursery) and therefore is open to change and experimentation. Corboy likes to say, "The farm grows vegetables and the nonprofit grows ideas." Two current ideas are a low-income CSA and a community kitchen in which Kensington residents can bake goods for sale or open small catering businesses and where cooking classes can be held. Corboy gives new projects like these three years to gauge whether they can work and if they fit into the overall farm. If they do both, they are folded into the Greensgrow operation at the end of the three years and new ideas are sought.

While nonprofits must spend much of their time applying for grants and meeting the stipulations of those grants, Corboy and Greensgrow, with their reliable "hard-money" income, can respond to the market and weave their way through the changing landscape of urban farming (such as developing a bee program on the same square footage occupied by the oil-conversion shed) without being tied to specific and finite sources of "soft money." Much of Greensgrow and The Philadelphia Project's long-term success must be attributed to the fact that they have a little bit of everything, and all of it is connected, somehow, as in any good, old city.

Farming in Kensington, now a low-income neighborhood largely of Russian and Irish immigrants, is no more new than farming is throughout Philadelphia. The city's community gardens, backyard gardens, and "guerrilla" gardens on vacant lots have been producing thousands of pounds of fresh food annually for over a century. The Vacant Lot Cultivation Association was founded in 1897, to help people access land and start market gardens. Food rationing during World War I and World War II spurred many Philadelphians, and Americans throughout the country, to plant gardens for food. And the exodus of African American farmers from the sharecropper South in the early to mid-twentieth century brought a new agrarian population to the city.

In the 1970s, the community vacant-lot gardens took off, just as the industrial boom imploded. Over one hundred thousand people lost their jobs, industries ran screaming, and many people bolted for the hills, or somewhere beyond Philly.

At the same time, another wave of southern African Americans moved north. They were joined by Puerto Ricans, who had begun arriving in small numbers during and after World War II and were now coming by the thousands, pushed by the transition of their island's economy from agriculture to export-oriented industry, and by Southeast Asians escaping the aftermath of the Vietnam War. Many of these newcomers came

The Greensgrow honey-bees add another source of income from farm sales, an additional item for CSA boxes, and pollinators for the nursery and farm.

from rural environments where they grew food or worked on farms. They brought an agricultural knowledge and ethic with them, though largely in the hands of the older generations. Ernesta Ballard of the Pennsylvania Horticultural Society launched the Philadelphia Green initiative in 1974, and Penn State began its Urban Gardening Program in 1977, a success that was eventually folded into a long-running U.S. Department of Agriculture program. According to a University of Pennsylvania report published by Domenic Vitiello and Michael Nairn in October 2009, both programs thrived, peaking in the 1990s with over two thousand projects that ranged the urban farm spectrum from gardens raising ornamental flowers to food-producing small farms.

The city agencies, meanwhile, took little interest in their landholdings and barely blinked at signing multiyear leases with neighborhood farmers for empty city lots. This opened the door to less-organized food production. The economic downturn of the 1970s made inner-city blight as American as apple pie. In Philly, pirate farmers built up soils and fed families and communities by pushing around a hoe. The commonsense food production continued into the 1990s. There weren't meetings or board members or conference calls. There was just a need for food, empty land, and people who knew how to dig in with a shovel and hoe.

Mary Seton Corboy originally placed the apiary on the roof-top of a shed to deter theft.

Even on a rainy afternoon, devoted customers come from all over Philadelphia to shop at the Greensgrow market.

Corboy calls a shovel "the idiot stick," and she holds it in high regard. She came onto the scene at the tail end of the late twentieth century's mini-urban agriculture revolution. Plenty of community and vacant-lot farms still exist from that time, but not on the scale they did thirty years ago. The decline is partly due to older farmers passing away and an evaporation of funds from Philadelphia Green, the U.S. Department of Agriculture, and Penn State's Urban Gardening Program. But other culprits include increased real-estate values, the subsequent interest of developers, and city agencies' reluctance to continue signing multiyear usage leases on the empty lots. The rogue farmers have had to abandon soils they had developed over the course of a decade or more.

So Corboy's success can be attributed to a new form of urban gardening, one with a hard-core commercial approach. Corboy is a gritty farmer with business savvy. She doesn't like meetings and she looks more comfortable in the bee suit and mask than she would in a tailored suit or a dress. When she takes off the bee outfit, she reveals a dusty, wrinkled Subaru farm shirt. Two Subaru wagons sit along the curb between the bee and tool lot and the larger farm and nursery. The socially progressive and locally based Subaru company sponsors Greensgrow.

Corboy and her cofounding partner, Tom Sereduk, started digging into the Kensington plot in 1998. The two entrepreneurs had restaurant experience and they saw a market for salad greens. They knew hydroponic growing methods (growing in mineral-enhanced water, rather than soil), which allowed them to bypass the immediate concerns over the lot's one-time Brownfields status (presence of hazardous contaminants), a distinction it had earned from the Environmental Protection Agency (EPA) following the closure of its former occupant, an industrial steel plant. Even though the EPA removed the contaminated soil and replaced it with clean backfill in 1993, the lot remained vacant for the next five years, until Corboy and Sereduk started Greensgrow. They were open only during the growing season, and they sold to white-tablecloth restaurants for a profit.

But kids threw rocks at them over the fence. Corboy and Sereduk were the energetic hippies who came into the neighborhood for half the year to grow fancy lettuce for fancy restaurants. They encountered an uphill battle to overcome the malevolence of some of the neighbors who didn't like the newcomers, a sentiment that disheartened Sereduk to the point that he ultimately left the garden. Corboy stuck with it and she and her budding staff kept the farm's vision going. "Over time, we never really invested in any one thing, so when the winds of change moved in—more and more interest in local foods—we shifted. We started growing more heirloom tomatoes and microgreens. Then we built the greenhouse, grew flowers, and stayed year-round, and the neighbors got interested. We saw what people grew in their pots here in the neighborhood, and we offered them in the nursery. As we've grown, we've tried to keep one foot in this community and one in the greater city."

At the corner of the farm, the chickens peck at the soil on one side of the chain-link fence and neighbors cruise on bikes or stroll the sidewalk a foot away. It's an easy symbol of the urban farm, but it actually does what you'd think it would: connect the community to a natural food source with that simple juxtaposition of concrete and soil. A few women sit on the steps of their row houses a block away. Their young kids bump Razor scooters over the sidewalk cracks, and they love the chickens.

Janice Teague has lived on the block for twenty-five years. She likes the farm. She goes every week to the Thursday market for fruit and vegetables, and she buys tomato plants to grow in her backyard garden, a six-by-two-foot sliver of soil in a tiny concrete-and-cinder-block patio. She doesn't have a car, so she can't get to Home Depot to buy potted plants. Greensgrow lets her use one of the farm's Subaru wagons to roll her purchases home, and the nursery prices are no more than Home Depot's or Lowe's.

"I'm not into the butter and milk and cheese stuff; I get that from the regular grocery store," says Teague. "My daughter gets her soap from the farm. I get fruit and bread and I get flowers that I plant in my backyard. I get peppers, cucumbers, tomatoes. They're fresher and they're a little more money, but I like Jersey tomatoes from the farm market better than the supermarket ones."

Teague says she doesn't see many neighbors at the Greensgrow market. The people she sees there are from elsewhere. The Thursday market shoppers reflect Teague's distinction that the shoppers aren't from the neighborhood. There are young, upwardly mobile professionals, mothers with strollers the size of a Peugeot, four friends carpooling in a Prius, a young lawyer in a suit, and a middle-aged woman in Birkenstocks. These are the typical locavores of our urban farm era. But there's also a policeman and the owner of the auto-detail shop across the street, so it's hard to stereotype too much, and the mix is encouraging.

Corboy has always intended for Greensgrow to be profitable. In fact, she wants it to be a model for sustainable profitability. As already mentioned, the nineteen staff members are paid by the for-profit side of the business, and the CSA, which is supplied by a large web of farms and producers with Greensgrow as the mothership distribution point, boasts four hundred members. That's a big number for a city-block farm. It's so big that Greensgrow has achieved the holy grail of the CSA model: a low-income option.

The low-income CSA is new, and it's a work in progress. The standard CSA model works like an investment: the member pays for his or her growing-season share in the farm up front, in March or April. This guarantees the member's investment in the farm and allows the farmer to know his or her budget for the year. Because the Greensgrow CSA has so many market-rate members (investors), it can buy in bulk from its network of eighty producers and thereby squeeze the low-income rate into the net sum of purchases. For instance, full-share, market-rate members pay $775 per year for twenty-four weeks of produce. (There are half shares for $435, delivered twice a month.) Those numbers crunch to roughly $32 per week. Low-income CSA members pay between $8 and $20 per share, delivered every other week. With so many members, Greensgrow can buy in bulk from certain growers. It is simple economics that allows farmers to charge slightly less for their product because they know the produce will be sold. On the other hand, Greensgrow can buy enough to supplement the low-income slice of their demand.

The challenge with the low-income scenario falls in the CSA's investment model. Many low-income community members buy food with Access cards, Philadelphia's version of food stamps. Since they receive the benefits every two weeks, many of them cannot pay the entire season's costs in one March or April payment. They have to pay with each share. So Erik Kintzel, Greensgrow's CSA manager who organizes the weekly shares' produce purchases from farmers and farm auctions, spends many hours on the phone.

Unfortunately, the low-income CSA is a great idea that might be ahead of its time. The slow-moving, large-scale health and human service programs can't keep up with the new food markets developing on hyperlocal levels in Philadelphia neighborhoods and around the country. If food stamps like Philadelphia's Access cards continue to be relied on to feed low-income families, then legislators must find a way to adapt them for use in burgeoning local food economies like Greensgrow.

It takes time, and Corboy has learned patience. It's been a dozen years since she ducked rocks while hanging plastic over the greenhouse. The bees help, but mainly she and her staff and her chickens and the nursery's petunias have put a face on the farm and the neighborhood. She has created a business and jobs, and her and the staff's forward momentum could lead to a shift in low-income food-service options. Luckily, Corboy isn't too immersed to miss the impact Greensgrow is making.

"In the short term I see a positive change. I got a Google alert last night. I don't usually check those, but I did this time. It was from a real-estate listing. It said, 'Great house, great location right next to Greensgrow Farm!!!' When you become an asset to your community or neighborhood, then you've done something. I don't do this just to be tan."

ESTABLISHED: 1998.

SIZE: One city block, plus a CSA network of eighty farms beyond Philadelphia.

MISSION: To reconnect city dwellers with rural food producers, to promote the greening of Philadelphia's homes and gardens, and to encourage social entrepreneurship through the use of vacant land.

WHO'S IN CHARGE: The Philadelphia Project oversees the executive director (Mary Seton Corboy) and nineteen employees.

SURROUNDING NEIGHBORHOOD: Kensington, a lower- to middle-class neighborhood made up predominantly of Irish and Russian Americans.

ZONING: "G-2" industrial.

FUNDING: Nursery, CSA, and farm market and restaurant sales bring in $1 million dollars annually; nonprofit funding from Subaru and individuals.

WHO EATS IT: Farm market consumers, four hundred market-rate CSA members, and low-income CSA members.

HOW TO Rehabilitate Contaminated Soils

If you grow salad greens in a backyard, you are getting the freshest possible produce at the best possible price. But how do you know if your soil has been contaminated with lead from paint chips? Or how do you know the soil isn't laced with toxic residue from a heavy-metal industry that was on the land decades before your home or farm was built?

Soil contamination is often the first obstacle encountered by urban farmers. Soil is the currency of the farm, and it's developed and enhanced over years of growth, decomposition, and renewal. Mary Corboy and Tom Sereduk started Greensgrow in a vacant lot in Philadelphia's Kensington neighborhood that, like many vacant lots in urban areas, was once used for industry. The Kensington plot's soil had been contaminated to the point of falling into the EPA's Brownfields status, and although the EPA had cleaned up the site, Corboy and Sereduk decided to eliminate any concerns about the soil quality by growing their produce hydroponically.

The Food Project, an urban farm in Boston, has a program specifically designed to help gardeners find out what's in their soil. The project's partnership with Wellesley College has enabled them to provide free soil tests to neighborhood gardeners and to experiment with several remediation strategies, including raised beds, compost amendment, excavation, and phytoremediation. They recommend compost amendment and raised beds as the most cost-effective and efficient remediation techniques.

In spring of 2007, the staff at the Jones Valley Urban Farm (page 91) transformed a vacant grass field in downtown Birmingham, Alabama, into a sea of sunflowers. They simply borrowed a tractor to till the soil and threw out a hundred pounds of seed. Two months later, the neighborhood had been transformed. The soil was better, the community was happier, and the sunflowers were sold to cover the farm's costs. Planting sunflowers helps clean up contaminated soil by putting it through the natural process known as phytoremediation, in which plants take up the contaminated soil in their tissue, and then the plants are removed and disposed of in a landfill. Even though a soil test had come back negative for dangerous levels of toxins, JVUF decided that a display of brilliant color culminating in a you-pick sunflower festival was a great way to start the new urban farm. Plus, after the harvest, the tilled sunflower stalks added vital nutrients to the soil.

Over the years, Jones Valley Urban Farm has been offered property from one side of the city to the other, ranging in size from a sliver of grass along an interstate to a twenty-five-acre field tucked inside a residential neighborhood. Regardless of the property, the first question always asked is what's living in the soil. If there has been no history of industrial use or contamination, the farm managers move on to other considerations, such as access to water and community interest. If there is a question about heavy-metal contamination, they send off soil samples for testing. The main concern is lead, which is a common contaminant in an industrial-based city like Birmingham. However, industrial use is only one of the many potential sources of contamination. The most frequent problems come from lead-based house paint chipping off of siding, and automobiles dripping oil or fuel.

Fortunately, there are many good options if contaminated soil is found. Greensgrow adopted the simplest technique for dealing with soil issues: avoid the soil. Their urban farm model focuses on growing nursery plants in greenhouses and "above-ground" vegetable production. Both systems leave the contaminated soil below the concrete, where it can't impact the edible plants.

Steps for Evaluating an Urban Farm Site for Contamination

DETERMINE THE LAND-USE HISTORY. Has the site been used for industrial purposes, such as hosting a gas station or laundromat? If so, address the soil quality with caution. The best way to research previous uses is to visit city hall with the property number in hand.

TEST THE SOIL. Most county extension services can do a basic soil test. If there is any reason to be suspicious based on the land-use history, seek out one of the private companies that specialize in heavy-metal contamination. Timberleaf Soil Testing provides a wide spectrum of soil analysis and consulting services (www.timberleafsoiltesting.com). Resource Center for Urban Agriculture has a Guide to Soil Contamination (www.ruaf.org/node/1003).

ASSESS YOUR OPTIONS. If the soil is contaminated at an unsafe level, you have a few options:

- Find a different location to farm. Most cities have an abundance of vacant land, and a different plot is often the most cost-effective approach.

- Grow plants in way that doesn't disturb the soil, such as in pots or raised beds. Added Value in Brooklyn, New York, farms an entire city block on top of the asphalt.

- Remediate the soil by physically removing the top layer, biologically altering the toxins, or chemically changing its composition. Before turning to remediation, consider the technique, time frame, effectiveness, and cost.

SEEK ADDITIONAL SUPPORT. There are a number of funding sources that assist organizations and individuals dealing with contaminated soil. Visit www.epa.gov for more information.

EAGLE STREET ROOFTOP FARM
BROOKLYN, NEW YORK

Eagle Street Rooftop Farm has its eye on Manhattan. Regardless of the fecundity of the kale or peppers or the clucking of the chickens inhabiting the six-thousand-square-foot roof, the visitor's gaze can't help but wander out, over the Hudson River, to an unimpeded view of the Manhattan skyline. But nowadays, it has become hard to tell whether the farm is looking at the city or the city is peering up at the farm.

Portraits of Annie Novak, Eagle Street's cofounder and director, and her farm have appeared in dozens of magazines and newspapers, and on television, such as CNN, the *New York Times*, and *New York* magazine. She is young, bright, and quirky-cool in her Huck Finn–chic farm attire, and she is passionate about the farm and its potential.

Novak would probably rather be farming than entertaining film crews, but so it goes on a project intended to be as much about education and outreach as it is about arugula, city chickens, and tomatoes. She runs the farm with the help of an intern, a few apprentices, and volunteers. They grow beautiful produce for sale at their Sunday market, via a small CSA, and to such high-end restaurants as Eat, Marlow & Sons, and Paulie Gee's. Finding locavores down the street is easy in food-savvy Brooklyn. And the produce carries enough value in this neighborhood to support the project as a for-profit endeavor. But Novak's vision extends far beyond her capabilities on the rooftop food island.

"We want to serve as a basis for potential," Novak says. "Everything we do here on a small scale can be blown up in any way. It's like a demo for everything. Because we're in New York, we have a broad reach. If I'm doing this in a city, I want to have that connection to as many people as possible. Otherwise, I'd rather just be farming in upstate New York."

Small farms and gardens, whether on rooftops or on the ground, reduce the amount of untreated water that pours into waterways and sewers when it rains.

The Eagle Street cabbage harvest.

Novak hopes that her outreach to school groups from Manhattan, New Jersey, the Bronx, Brooklyn, and Queens and to anyone who walks up the warehouse stairs to buy a bundle of radishes or four eggs will promote an awareness of local, healthy food. "The whole point of this project was to get people so excited about food that they would support our upstate farms as consumers," she says. The surprise factor—growing in the city is a surprise and growing on a roof is an even bigger surprise—helps to shock people into considering the origins of their food and the possibilities for seeking out good sources, whether from a city rooftop or an upstate farmer.

In a way, Eagle Street, and even Novak herself, represents one of the ways in which urban farms consciously act as seeds to the greater goal of a fundamentally new perspective on food. Novak knows she cannot grow enough vegetables or produce enough eggs on the roof of one partially empty warehouse in Brooklyn to feed even the immediate neighborhood. But she capitalizes on the spotlight the farm receives as a means of generating interest in rooftop farming in metro New York and informing her consumers, visitors, students, and her much larger fan base about the availability of fresh, local food entering the city from upstate New York farms. She's also aware, as are all urban farmers in this book, of the chance to grow new farmers via internships and volunteer work.

Eagle Street sells produce straight off the roof on Sundays and has also part-nered with a young upstate farmer to enhance the rooftop's CSA offerings.

Annie Novak with one of her chickens at the Eagle Street Rooftop Farm in Brooklyn.

Karen Turner is an Eagle Street intern. She wants to farm one hundred acres in Texas. Her family has lived on ten acres near San Antonio for a long time, and she plans to start her farm on that land, probably with something simple like chickens and fruit trees and vegetables. Eventually, she'd like to have a dairy.

But at age twenty-five, Karen is in Brooklyn. She works among the rows of kale, sprinkling coffee grounds at the base of the stalks. The grounds come from a five-gallon bucket that she carried from a neighborhood café up two flights of stairs to the warehouse roof. Aphids are attacking the kale and something has to be done, organically of course. Someone at the farm had read that spent coffee grounds are a cheap, effective way to deter the aphids and save the kale. The distant Empire State Building seems to poke out from behind Karen's straw hat. We're a long way from Texas in every way except for her hat, the soil, the sun's mid-June, southern-style intensity, and the farm culture.

Eagle Street is Karen Turner's first experience growing food. She worked with livestock for a week in Arkansas via a Heifer International farm stay. "For the first time, during that farm stay," she says, "I felt I was where I was supposed to be. And then I really came to that conclusion a month ago, here at Eagle Street."

Karen heard of Eagle Street through her master's program in food studies at New York University. Agriculture, horticulture, and their cross-disciplinary place in urban planning, public policy, and engineering departments is becoming a more common course offering in colleges and universities, another indication of the growing interest in a new food system and hope for a broadened sustainable food industry. Karen's father died when she was young, so the family farm, long managed by her mother, grows only hay now. She says the land is capable of supporting the biodiverse, intensive farm she wants to start after she learns the ropes and feels comfortable at the helm of her own farm business.

But in Brooklyn, she's in full training mode, reading books about farming and planting at night and practicing new skills with Novak on the roof by day. "Monday I helped build the third pallet compost bin, and that's the system I'll need in Texas. Everything gets me pumped right now. I can't wait to do all of this when I get home."

Admittedly, rooftop gardens and "living roofs" are chic, especially in food-hip Brooklyn. But the benefits of these unique growing spaces are becoming more widely recognized: reduced heating and cooling bills for the building and reduced overall temperature from a city's "heat island effect." Poor soils in metro New York and most

other cities mean a rooftop acts as a sort of massive raised bed with clean, organic soil for food growth. But another reason rooftop farms fit into the overall urban farm spectrum has to do with available land. Cities like New York and Chicago have relatively few vacant lots, and the empty land that does exist has a high real-estate value that inhibits the owner, be it the city or an individual, from giving over valuable property for food growth. Detroit and Birmingham have plenty of flat warehouse rooftops, but with so much empty land on the ground, the motivation for rooftop farming is reduced.

In some ways, the rooftop garden is the poster child for urban farming: clean, beautiful, with views, and atop the very thing that makes a city a city: big buildings with flat roofs. Its aesthetic and conceptual efficiency make it an appealing vehicle for promoting the growing of food in an urban environment. And, in a way, Eagle Street is the poster child for the rooftop garden. It highlights the vital role that urban farms, especially high-profile ones like Eagle Street, play in the marketing of the new

The farm adds value by providing yoga classes and other special gatherings that draw more awareness to the garden.

123

agriculture movement and the transformation of our food systems. Growing produce almost becomes secondary to attracting visitors to a beautiful rooftop farm with a world-class view where they can see, touch, and learn about their food's origin. It's better than a Times Square billboard.

ESTABLISHED: 2009.

SIZE: One-half acre.

MISSION: To grow good food, educate good eaters, and provide an outstanding example of the utility of green roofs as a community base, green space, and site of ecological change.

WHO'S IN CHARGE: Farm director (Annie Novak) who manages four apprentices and volunteer interns.

SURROUNDING NEIGHBORHOOD: Greenpoint, Brooklyn.

ZONING: Industrial.

FUNDING: The green roof was installed by Goode Green and paid for by Broadway Stages. Seasonal seeds are purchased by the CSA members. Produce sales provide staff pay. Educational programming is sponsored by Growing Chefs, a nonprofit.

WHO EATS IT: Six area restaurants, fifteen CSA shareholders, and hundreds of locavore visitors.

HOW TO Convert Rooftops to Residential Gardens and Urban Farms

The green roof has been around for centuries, as evidenced by the old homes and barns in European towns and countryside. The modern version of the manufactured living roof evolved in Germany in the 1960s, and it has taken a few modern steps in its last half century of engineering. The steps are simple and green roofs will certainly continue to become more efficient and affordable as the young technology matures.

Today, landmark living roofs sit atop the city hall buildings of Chicago, Atlanta, Seattle, and Toronto and on the U.S. Department of Agriculture's Whitten Building in Washington, D.C. Governments and corporations see long-term dollar savings in the energy-conservation numbers of green roofs, plus there's the added bonus of good PR when you grow organic food on your building. With the increasing attraction of farm-to-plate food items on many restaurant menus, especially in progressive cities like New York, entrepreneurs are looking at rooftop farms as opportunities for social and economic benefit.

The largest rooftop farm in America was completed in 2010, across town from Eagle Street, in Queens. Ben Flanner, who cofounded Eagle Street with Annie Novak, developed the idea after leaving Eagle Street. Brooklyn Grange occupies an acre, or 40,000 square feet, atop a 1919 building. It holds 1.2 million pounds of soil, or 30 pounds per square foot. In its first summer, it is estimated the farm produced 16,000 pounds of fruits and vegetables for sale at markets and to restaurants.

In other words, rooftop farms are not just a feel-good, look-good architectural gimmick. And it's not too crazy to imagine flying into a city in ten years and seeing a puzzle of green patches with hoop houses and chicken coops coloring in the once-dreary rooftops. Indeed, don't be surprised if you find yourself falling asleep underneath the roots of your salad in the not-too-distant future.

Sometimes the most challenging part is determining whether the initial cost of constructing the green roof will be worthwhile in the long term, so we include three reasons, economic and conservation based, for taking the plunge.

Three Reasons to Go Green Roof

Green-roof installations are pricey, ranging from ten to fifty dollars per square foot, but there are significant economic and societal benefits that offset the cost.

LONG-TERM SAVINGS. An average roof's waterproofing membrane must be replaced every fifteen to twenty years because of exposure to ultraviolet rays and the thermal expansion and contraction that result from constant heating and cooling. Green roofs have proven to extend the life of the waterproof membrane by a multiple of four. A well-insulated home or building can save 30 percent on heating and cooling bills by reducing heat loss in winter and heat absorption in summer.

URBAN HEAT REDUCTION. Regular roofs, especially those covered in dark materials, absorb heat from the sun and act as hot stones, emitting that heat into the immediate environment. According to the Environmental Protection Agency, the resulting overall "heat island effect" of a city of one million people can raise daytime temperatures up to 5.4°F and evening temperatures up to a shocking 22°F over temperatures in surrounding areas. Green roofs dissipate that heat and often create microenvironments that are actually cooler than the surrounding air temperatures.

STORM-WATER REDUCTION. As more and more pavement is laid in cities, less water is absorbed into the ground and more enters an often outdated sewage system, resulting in water-treatment plant malfunctions and more costs to the taxpayer in terms of utility services. Green roofs capture up to 70 percent of the rain that falls on them. Many municipalities are offering incentives for the installation of green roofs, largely because of the storm-water management improvements. Receiving approval for a building permit in the city of Chicago generally takes up to two years. But if the building incorporates a green roof, the city guarantees permit evaluation within thirty days. New York offers four dollars per square foot toward the installation of a green roof.

How to Build a Green Roof

Constructing a green roof is simply a matter of adding the right layers, in the correct order. The first step, of course, is to have an engineer evaluate your building to ensure the structure can support the added weight of soil. Once you get the go-ahead, there are six simple steps, in layers, to a green roof.

MEMBRANE. All roofs have a waterproof membrane. Living roofs build on the original membrane with the following series of geotextile membranes.

ROOT BARRIER. This layer rests atop the waterproof membrane to protect the roof from damage due to penetrating roots.

DRAINAGE LAYER. An absorbent layer, this egg-crate-type plastic material has tiny holes between the cups. Water absorbed from rain and watering either drains through the holes and runs off the waterproof membrane, or collects in the cups and eventually evaporates back into the root layer.

SILT SCREEN. The drainage layer is interwoven with a silt screen to keep the soil from eroding and to suspend the egg-crate system off the roof so water can drain.

WATER RETENTION MAT. This is usually a fleece-type layer that absorbs the initial water seepage from the soil and keeps it in the system, via evaporation, longer.

SOIL. The amount and type of soil depends on the intended use of the green roof. A simple, often residential-style roof of low-maintenance, shallow-root plants, such as decorative succulents and leafy greens (kale, chard, broccoli), can require as little as six inches of soil. Larger-production rooftop projects require about eighteen inches of soil that is finely crushed to make it denser and therefore heavy.

CATHERINE FERGUSON ACADEMY
DETROIT, MICHIGAN

Avram Rodgers, age six, says he's a secret agent. He hustles to the rabbit pins in the back of a fenced-in, grassy area at the Catherine Ferguson Academy farm. A few ducks waddle in a little pool in the center of the enclosure. Goats chew grass in an enclosure thirty feet away, and a group of young women students build a small greenhouse fifty feet away.

Avram points out an eviscerated rabbit in the thick grass and says that he must find its killer. The young bunny likely escaped its cage and a hawk or raccoon is the obvious suspect. But Avram is less certain. He investigates the crime scene for only thirty seconds more. Then his youthful imagination takes a turn, and he veers out of the duck and rabbit area toward the greenhouse.

Although he doesn't find the culprit, Avram has just revealed something far more interesting. His backyard mystery personifies the collision of life and death and wide-open imagination that has come to define Detroit in a much deeper way than headlines about joblessness and brutal images of windowless buildings.

By definition, Avram is a city kid from Detroit, but he walks around this farm like a country kid. He grew up on the urban produce and livestock farm that takes up roughly half of the school lot for the Catherine Ferguson Academy, a Detroit school for teenage mothers. Avram's mother, Ashley Rodgers, entered Catherine Ferguson in the ninth grade, after becoming pregnant with Avram.

Ashley, who is now twenty-one, leads the crew of students as they wrap the small greenhouse in plastic. The group of girls, mostly age fifteen to nineteen, will travel to South Africa at the end of July for an international youth conference on food security and farming. They'll teach a workshop in greenhouse construction and learn other

Teacher Paul Weertz has created a one-of-a-kind curriculum that combines hands-on farm experience with classroom science for students such as the one shown here.

techniques from fellow international students of agriculture. As unlikely as it may sound outside of this garden, some of America's youthful farm ambassadors will come from the heart of Detroit.

Detroit is our contemporary model for city-wide economic collapse. In 2010, its unemployment and home foreclosure rates were the highest in the country. The city has become the national symbol of unemployment and industrial failure just as Wall Street has become the national symbol for greed and excess. But Detroit is also like a gritty blank slate. For decades, traced back to the race riots of the 1940s and 1960s, the inner city has been left to fend for itself as most of the wealthy residents and their tax base migrated to the suburbs or out of the state. The population, which peaked at 2 million in 1950, now hovers at 850,000. The exodus of industrial laborers left behind an estimated seventeen thousand acres of vacant lots.

Detroit's sea of potential has created a sense of Manifest Destiny among urban farm pioneers. Just like artists who experiment at the fringe of their crafts when they move into huge, unwanted warehouse spaces in empty downtowns, Detroit farmers are at the cutting edge of urban agriculture.

Umbrella organizations like The Greening of Detroit have amassed a network of unused land and reclaimed it for tree nurseries, fruit-tree orchards, and small, intensive vegetable gardens. Begun in 1989, initially to plant new trees in response to decades of massive tree loss (a half million lost between 1950 and 1980), the Greening now has its hands in hundreds of community gardens and small plots throughout the city, in addition to its large tree-planting projects, like the 105 acres at Rouge Park.

Detroit is a wild fringe of urban renewal, community organizing, and do-gooder land grabbing. On the fringe of that fringe stands the Catherine Ferguson Academy (CFA). The CFA farm has been flying under the radar for twenty years, and it's been able to remain out of Detroit's current frenzied climate of community building and competition that has resulted from so much available land and so many green ideas. CFA is just a school with a farm, and that simplicity and focus might be why it has survived and evolved to such a sophisticated level.

The CFA farm did not begin with a mission to save the city or to be a model for the world. It began because Paul Weertz, a science teacher at the academy, did not want his students—teenage mothers and mothers-to-be—to inhale formaldehyde during dissections. Even traces of the chemical can harm a fetus. So Weertz, now fifty-six, began keeping a couple of live rabbits and chickens in pens out back. He

Avram Rodgers hangs out while his mom and her classmates construct a greenhouse behind the Catherine Ferguson Academy.

could practice "fresh dissections" without the need for toxic preservatives. Soon, he had more chickens and rabbits and a few goats. Weertz and his students planted apple trees in the old playground and slowly built up from there. Within fifteen years, they had plowed the land and built a fence, a small barn, and then a big barn for hay and for milking the goats. It all grew slowly and always with the help of the students.

"The students come here pretty beat up," Weertz says. "[Because of the teenage pregnancy,] their parents are mad at them, their boyfriends are mad, their teachers [are] mad. The girls are angry and hurt. So one of the things I like to do right away is build them up. I'll bring them out to the tractor. I'll get a student on it and tell her about the clutch and start it up and boom! They get scared and think they can't do it. The clutch jerks and the tractor moves forward—at about two miles an hour—and then you can just see them go from slumped over and scared to sitting up straight, like *I'm driving a tractor*. After they do these powerful things—drive a tractor, control a horse, milk a goat—they realize they can handle some of the difficult things in life that they're faced with. They can stand up to a man or talk to their parents."

Paul Weertz has successfully integrated daily farmwork into his alternative science curriculum.

Weertz is old school. He talks in a folksy manner full of practicality and commonsense truisms. He seems like a teacher transplanted into twenty-first-century Detroit from the early-twentieth-century prairie.

"We [teachers] have to compete with the computers and the actors and actresses," he says. "*Planet Earth*—I have to compete with that? There's just one of me up here. But we as educators can make it real."

Weertz spends about half his class time in the classroom and half at the farm, overseeing the students as they milk the goats, feed the chickens or the horse, or water and weed and seed the vegetable plots. They seed, collect, and bale hay from ten acres of vacant city lots and then store the hay in the barn.

"The farm is a great way to teach parenting skills," he says. "If you don't water and feed the plants, they wither and die. And training the goats for milking is a great lesson, too. We teach kids how training works—you have to be smarter than the animal. I let the goats run wild for the first milking and then I teach the girls that you have to outthink them and train them to do what you want them to do."

In 2010, *Atlantic Monthly* published an article entitled "Cultivating Failure." The author argues that the recently vogue school farms act as a distraction from the book learning and standardized test preparations that must occur to get our underserved students into college and therefore a higher economic strata.

Weertz gets that occasionally, as well, even in Detroit, where growing your own food is becoming a powerful symbol of autonomy. "Some people say I just have them out there working on the farm, but I think they're getting smarter. Many kids are just not moving [nowadays], and scientists are learning that we're pretty smart when we use our hands. I think when we're out there working with our hands, we're recharging our brains.

"If I said to a farm kid, 'You don't need computers, you just need to know farm equipment,' that'd be discriminating. You can't do the inverse with the city kids and tell them all they need to know is on a computer."

The system of standardized testing relies heavily on classroom skills, but the farm, via feeding schedules, planting plans, and chicken-coop measurements, puts those skills to real tests. Weertz uses the farm every day in his science classes. At the beginning of the semester, the students employ the scientific method to devise a hypothesis involving the farm. For example, does a bigger egg yield a bigger chicken? Or, does milk production go up or down in cold weather? Students spend part of every two-hour class collecting data for their research project, which, by the end of the semester, they will have completed. Thanks to the livestock, Weertz uses the farm through the winter. Students milk goats, collect chicken eggs, manage the hay in the barn, and grow produce in a hoop house. Other classes use the farm, as well. Art and writing projects often incorporate the outdoor setting, and the Spanish teacher sometimes places signs on the barn for vocabulary exercises.

The Edible Schoolyard, which originated in Berkeley, California, is frequently described as the school-farm model for America. It has merit and works especially well in the Bay Area, where a long growing season coincides with most of the school year. But one of the major roadblocks to education reform is trying to fit a model that works in one place or one school onto a totally different social, fiscal, and physical environment. The CFA program operates in its own world, an alternative space of rejected students in a rejected city. Weertz never asked permission beyond his immediate boss, Principal Asenath Andrews. Andrews arrived at the school in 1985, and her efforts to secure funding explain much of the school's unique success.

Students milking a goat in the barn that they helped build.

But creating an urban farm in a city school is not easy. Safety regulations, funding, standardized-test requirements, liability issues, and anxious parents are the obvious obstructions to putting a working produce and livestock farm on the back lot of every high school. But it's working on one block of Detroit. Perhaps the best lesson from CFA is its one-of-a-kind, place-based approach to responding to the needs of its unique student population.

Ashley Rodgers graduated from the academy in spring 2010 and worked at the school and farm over the summer. Next fall, she will attend Wayne County Community College, but she won't be studying agriculture. She wants to be a nurse and she wants to travel the world, taking Avram with her.

Detroit is America's closest thing to a laboratory. The Catherine Ferguson Academy is just a school with a farm out back. But all of it—the city, the farm, the school, the hands-on nature of the farm as classroom—is a successful experiment.

Note: In June 2011, CFA was nearly shut down by a Detroit school district budget cut. It was saved by Evans Solutions, a for-profit group that will operate CFA as a charter school. Time will tell what impact the change will have on the school and the farm.

ESTABLISHED: 1990.

SIZE: 1 acre.

MISSION: To ensure that every student completes her high school education and is conferred with a state of Michigan endorsement. Each young woman must obtain the skills necessary to be a competent, caring mother and to support herself and her family.

WHO'S IN CHARGE: Principal (Asenath Andrews), science teacher (Paul Weertz), plus support from The Greening of Detroit staff.

SURROUNDING NEIGHBORHOOD: Lower- and middle-income single-family homes and apartments, many abandoned.

ZONING: Institutional.

FUNDING: Detroit Board of Education and the State of Michigan.

WHO EATS IT: Students and shoppers at city farmer's markets.

HOW TO Raise Urban Livestock

Instead of a dusty ball field, the Catherine Ferguson Academy has one horse, five goats, thirty chickens, ten rabbits, five ducks, and hundreds of thousands of bees on its school lot. The students move comfortably among the animals and they care for the livestock every day. More than likely, they had never seen a live chicken before they arrived at the school, much less built a hay barn, driven a tractor, or harnessed a horse.

Although livestock in the city may seem odd today, it was not that unusual a century ago. Only in the last fifty years have farm animals become taboo and even illegal in many U.S. cities. The Catherine Ferguson Academy is, of course, an educational institution. Just as nearby Wayne State University can accommodate guinea pigs and fish for research and lab purposes on its campus, the academy keeps their animals under the same laws. The desire among urban farmers and community and backyard gardeners to raise livestock is growing, however. In her book *Farm City*, Novella Carpenter made famous the trials and tribulations of homesteading livestock in her Oakland, California, neighborhood. It just made sense to her to raise animals in her backyard, so one day she started doing it, and has been advocating for urban livestock farming ever since.

The move to outlaw livestock and farming in cities was not motivated by some conspiracy to oppress farmers. Instead, it was a by-product of our society embracing the idea of transference of germs first put forth by Louis Pasteur in the mid-nineteenth century. Our health departments have tried to separate the source of contamination (animal manure) from high concentrations of people. Taken to its logical conclusion, we now have a society that has specific places for people, specific places for animals, and specific places for vegetable production.

The unintended consequence of this, however, is a society philosophically disconnected from its food system. This has led directly to generations of children unaware of where their food comes from and therefore making poor dietary choices. It has also led to an overreliance on antibiotics in an attempt to compensate for the ecological imbalance on our nation's farms. Urban farmers around the country are pushing the pendulum back toward regulations that are in closer alignment with ecological thinking.

How to Change Your City's Livestock Policy

Here are a handful of simple efforts citizens can make toward effecting urban livestock policy change in their communities.

EASE INTO IT. Policy makers are much more likely to support changes to urban livestock zoning if the revisions are relatively minor and simple. Legalizing a small number of hens without roosters for a backyard is an easy win. From there, build a coalition.

BUY LOCAL. Every time you eat, you vote. When you buy sustainably produced food from local sources, you are voting for more local sources. With a greater market demand, more and more farmers will work to increase the supply. As both the supply and the demand grow, policy makers will take notice.

ENCOURAGE THE LOCAL PRESS TO DOCUMENT THE BENEFITS OF A VIABLE LOCAL FOOD ECONOMY. Writing editorials about possible changes to urban livestock policy and promoting press around existing barriers is the first step toward getting things changed.

SUPPORT LOCAL SCHOOL PROGRAMS THAT GET STUDENTS ONTO FARMS. The underlying cause for our dysfunctional food system is simple: children aren't growing up connected to the source of their food, so they don't have any interest in improving it. Ensuring that all children, but especially urban youth, clearly understand the connection between their lives and the source of their sustenance is essential for a vibrant, sustainable food system.

The Best Livestock for a City

CHICKENS. Every backyard needs some hens. Leave the roosters, however, to the rural farms. You don't need a rooster for egg production, and your neighbors will find much less to complain about. Hens produce two eggs every three days, so you don't need many for a continuous supply of fresh eggs.

GOATS. Keep goats away from anything you don't want chewed up, like house siding. Do put them near any overgrowth you want contained. They love to eat things like kudzu and blackberries that often plague vacant urban lots.

RABBITS. Probably the best urban livestock to raise because of their size and quiet nature, rabbits generate great manure for compost piles. Plus, they are not messy or dirty animals, which means their hutches are easy to keep clean. Grass-based pellet-ized feed is widely available and affordable.

GUINEA PIGS. Considered a staple part of the diet in many South American cities, guinea pigs are easy to raise in an urban environment. They are fast breeders, too, which means they can be a profitable enterprise for an urban farmer even on a small scale. Raising guinea pigs is similar to raising rabbits in terms of cages and feeding.

BEES. With a little study and some basic materials, anyone can keep bees. The hives should be placed away from children, so put them on a roof or inside a fenced area. The return for your investment will be delicious honey and an increased yield in your veg-etables and fruits.

For great build-your-own chicken-coop designs, go to www.backyardchickens.com. For manufactured kid-friendly bee houses and accessories, chicken coops, rabbit hutches, and guinea pig pens, go to www.omlet.us.

enhouse. He looks enormous
e a day away from being sold at
shoulders, and tattooed arms bulge
boxer. Melvin and a dozen other interns
an Farm in the Englewood neighborhood
ings from April through October they weed,
W.   arket shares on the farm, then move indoors to
the r.   om. The men and women spend the afternoon in
worksho   sons in soil preparation to financial planning.

Ten years   s rebuilding houses in the same Englewood neighborhood.
He remembers h.   hire men to watch his house projects at night so vagrants
wouldn't steal the new windows, doors, or plumbing he had installed. Back then,
Melvin never thought about growing food, and he never worried seriously about being
homeless or drowning in debt. He thinks about all three now.

The crash of the real-estate market in 2008 hit Melvin Price especially hard. The
forty-five-year-old builder and carpenter had been making a good living in Chicago
for years. He bought a house in the New City neighborhood. Because the house had
burned, he got it for $4,000, put in about $15,000 in repairs, and hoped to sell or
rent it. An appraiser put the new value at $145,000. He couldn't believe it, not in that
neighborhood, but he was convinced enough to reject an offer of $85,000, holding
out for more. The promise of the upward spiral of home ownership still had legs at
the time.

Melvin Price graduated
from the Growing Home
program in 2010.

Then he turned his sights on Camden, New Jersey. He had visited the town and seen the glut of dirt-cheap homes that could be fixed up easily. He refinanced his New City property and bought two adjacent homes in Camden for $20,000 total, intending to rehab them, with the help of a buddy, for a quick turnaround. But when Melvin showed up in Camden a month or so after the online purchase, the houses had been demolished by the city and he was left with the $30,000 demolition fee.

Spiking interest rates on the shoddy mortgage he had signed for the house back in New City raised his mortgage to $1,700 per month, forcing Melvin to foreclose. One too many hard knocks and Melvin was back in Chicago, where the carpentry work had dried up and he had a dumpster of debt.

Melvin's story, unfortunately, is a common one from the housing recession of the late 2000s. He made risky decisions and they caught up to him. But the atmosphere of the late 1990s and early to mid-2000s was one of unbridled potential in real-estate speculation and rehab. With the subprime mortgage implosion of 2008 and the subsequent recession, many people like Melvin skidded off the tightrope of equity and debt they had laid out for themselves. Melvin, then, represents many Americans' surprising proximity to unemployment and even homelessness.

Melvin read about Growing Home on the Internet and was surprised to discover that there was a farm in the Englewood neighborhood. He also saw that Growing Home offered a paid internship. So Melvin and nineteen other interns (some of whom moved into other jobs during the summer) began the 2010 growing season together in April. The men and women come from diverse backgrounds. Some are directed to the program by mental-health workers and social workers. The majority (70 percent of this year's class), however, are referred by their parole officers.

Growing Home is a farm and a job, but it's also a training program. The interns work in the greenhouses for three hours each morning, Tuesday through Friday. After lunch, they participate in classroom workshops on job training skills. The results are layered. For one, Englewood benefits from the adaptive reuse of what was an abandoned lot and has become a beautiful, productive farm that can operate year-round thanks to the greenhouses. Second, the interns learn gardening and job skills, receive direction into full-time work, and get to eat healthy food. And last, Chicago has another source of fresh produce. The vegetables are sold at the Green City Market in Lincoln Park and at the Englewood market, which offers a new food option in a community of seventy thousand residents and only one major grocery store.

Harry Rhodes helped start Growing Home in 2001. He's seen it ascend from an idea into a successful, award-winning project whose numbers tell the story. "Over 150 people have gone through the program," says Harry. "About 65 percent move into employment or educational training and 90 percent find stable housing. The recidivism rate in Illinois is over 50 percent (within three years of release). Our program has seen a 5 percent recidivism rate. It shows that when people are given a chance to work and change their lives, they will do everything they can to stay out of prison."

Beth Gunzel directs Growing Home's job training program. She says the farm and classroom complement each other, allowing the trainees to develop not only work-site skills, but also a résumé and letters of recommendation. But more than anything, having a job in a safe environment provides the most effective, if simple, benefit.

"One of the main components in recidivism," says Gunzel, "is people not having jobs. Although we don't measure causation or correlation, we can observe that when people have jobs they are motivated not to get involved in something that could get them into trouble. The felonies we're seeing are largely survival mechanisms, crimes that generate money in illegal ways."

Director Harry Rhodes and a trainee harvest produce for a Chicago farmer's market.

Hoop houses allow Growing Home to extend the season despite Chicago's harsh winter climate.

Melvin's surprise at the presence of a working production farm, a beautiful green space, in the middle of the Englewood neighborhood's downtrodden landscape illustrates the benefits of the farm that extend beyond the group of interns. Growing Home has transformed a bleak scene at Wood Street into a safe, cared-for enclave that grows over ten thousand pounds of fresh food on two-thirds of an acre each year. Building on the success of the plot, the farm has expanded its mission to include a community task force of neighborhood aldermen and councilmen. They hope to spread farming as a business model for potential backyard and vacant-lot growers in the neighborhood. Growing Home can provide the tools and knowledge to support these new enterprises. Melvin brings his construction tools to Wood Street for regular maintenance and construction needs. He and many other staff and interns have the knowledge and skills to help Englewood residents create their own food gardens.

Growing Home offers a shining example of how the urban farm can fill a role as a powerful social-service outlet. While the Homeless Garden Project (HGP) in Santa Cruz (page 25) and Growing Home focus on different demographics—HGP works with homeless adults and Growing Home aims to reach the formerly incarcerated—they are in the same place on the urban farm and new agriculture spectrum. HGP and Growing Home are social service programs that use a farm as their medium of instruction and training. The farms are merely the launching pad back into productive society.

Harry echoes the lament of Paul and Darrie at HGP about the challenges of balancing high-quality organic food production with on-the-job training of workers new to agriculture. But it's the combination of those two things, learning and producing, that can be the powerful engine behind the surface beauty of a calm, green space amid urbanity.

William Harris, forty, is another intern. He works the Green City Market on Saturday morning. It bustles with people and the market stands are piled high with carrots, beets, chard, arugula, tomatoes, cheeses, breads, jams, and meats from farmers and artisans based on the outskirts of Chicago and deep in farm country. William is one of two interns working Growing Home's market on a Saturday in 2010. The staff rotates each market. William's parole officer directed him to Growing Home and he didn't know what to think. He'd spent seven years in prison and didn't have a clue about gardening.

"I didn't come into this program with the idea of liking gardening, but I really do now," William says. "I'm in dental assistant school beginning in the fall, but I plan to own a small business on the side of that career. I'll do landscaping and make gardens in people's backyards."

Melvin has ideas, too. He's talked about starting a catfish farm and selling the fish in Englewood and elsewhere. He thinks they'd go like hotcakes in the neighborhood. He also wants to get back into the business he knows: home building and carpentry.

"Now I'm just trying to save enough money to get a house here," Melvin says. "They sell them for seven thousand dollars. I want to get something and sit on it for five to seven years. Fix it and rent it. This housing market will come back.

At Growing Home's Wood Street Urban Farm, tomatoes grow much further into the fall thanks to the hoop houses.

Rainbow chard grows well throughout the summer in both back-yards and hoop houses.

"I wish there were more jobs like this [farm] in the city. It's relaxing—you've got to be dedicated to this. I'm not in it for the money, but the people out here are so at ease. We love what we're doing."

ESTABLISHED: 2001.

SIZE: Two-thirds of an acre.

MISSION: To operate, promote, and demonstrate the use of organic agriculture as a vehicle for job training, employment, and community development.

WHO'S IN CHARGE: Executive director (Harry Rhodes), board of directors (Valerie Denney, president), advisory council, and thirteen staff overseeing up to twenty interns.

SURROUNDING NEIGHBORHOOD: The Englewood neighborhood on the south side of Chicago.

ZONING: Wood Street Urban Farm, M2–1.

FUNDING: Private foundations, government, corporations, small businesses, and individual donors.

WHO EATS IT: Englewood and New City residents via the Wood Street Farm Stand and Englewood Farmers Market, uptown city residents via the Green City Market, and one hundred CSA members.

HOW TO Extend the Growing Season with Hoop Houses and Greenhouses

Going through the door to a greenhouse in Chicago in February is like stepping into a tropical paradise. The warm smell of soil and plants with a touch of humidity is in stark contrast to the frigid temperatures outside. Rows of seedlings stretch skyward, each promising a bounty of wonderful food. But growing edible plants in winter requires some help. The good news is that most people like to eat year-round, even when the ground is frozen solid. That means there's a market waiting for urban farmers savvy enough to figure out how to keep their plants alive.

The other good news is that this consistent market opens a door to creating financially viable businesses in the city, instead of just a community gentrification project. Mary Corboy, from Philadelphia's Greensgrow (page 103), sees this clearly. "Season extension with greenhouses and hoop houses is an important part of the small producer's business model," she says. "If you're working on an acre, you need to figure out how to maximize that land year-round. An important part of the business strategy is to work with a customer base year-round."

But in most parts of the country, you can't produce salable products all year long without some help. Greenhouses and other season-extending techniques become a vital part in a project's potential success, and they're easy to construct. The students at Catherine Ferguson Academy in Detroit put one up during a week of science classes.

Four Ways to Extend the Growing Season

GREENHOUSES. Covered with either plastic or glass, greenhouses use a heat source, such as a furnace, to keep temperatures between 50° and 90°F. With proper ventilation, they provide an ideal environment to start seedlings for transplanting outdoors. Because it's easier to create ideal conditions for seed germination (moisture, temperature, protection from predators) in greenhouses, the germination rate is increased and the health of seedlings is improved. This means a farmer can produce more plants faster with the same-sized farm, translating to higher yields and more profits.

Greenhouses also allow a farmer to grow plants for harvest during the winter. Salad greens and other leafy crops are ideal for greenhouse production and can be highly profitable. Potted plants, such as herbs and vegetables, can also be lucrative in an urban market.

HIGH TUNNELS. Similar to greenhouses, but without supplemental heat or ventilation, high tunnels rely on trapping the sun's energy underneath the covering and then releasing the heat throughout the night. They are ideal for farmers with field-scale operations who want to extend the growing season, either by starting crops earlier or continuing to grow them later than the climate would normally allow.

High tunnels use adjustable sides to keep temperatures cool during the day. In the afternoon, the sides and ends are closed to trap the sun's heat. This is a low-cost way to increase yields and therefore profits. To avoid late-spring frosts, tomatoes are often transplanted into a high tunnel a month before they can be planted outside. This allows a farmer to have earlier fruit for sale, usually at a time when other producers don't have fruit yet and the prices are higher.

COLD FRAMES. Like high tunnels but on a smaller scale, cold frames are usually plastic-covered frames placed over seedlings and plants outdoors. They trap the sun's energy during the day and then release it during the night. Cold frames must be physically opened and closed each day, but they can be an affordable way to start seedlings in the winter and to grow plants throughout the year in cool climates.

FROST CLOTHS. Made from either spun plastic or cloth, these sheets can be pulled over rows of plants when temperatures are expected to drop below freezing. The fabric is designed to let air in and out and to let most of the sunlight in. The soil temperature increases and the leaves are protected from cold winds, so the plants grow normally. Frost cloths are an affordable way to increase the rate of a plant's growth and protect it from predators, such as birds or moths.

Pennywise Methods for Heating a Greenhouse

Just as with all aspects of a farming business, the benefits of these season-extending methods must be balanced with their costs. A greenhouse can be expensive to keep warm and ventilated, easily costing a farmer as much as, if not more than, the increased profits from extending the season. Finding affordable sources of heat is critical. Here are three pennywise sources.

WOOD CHIPS. Many urban farms can easily locate free sources for wood chips, which can then be used to heat a greenhouse efficiently. Some municipalities have ordinances that prevent burning of wood, so check local regulations first.

VEGETABLE OIL. Again, many urban farms can find free sources for used vegetable oil that can either be filtered and then burned or turned into biodiesel and then burned.

COMPOST. Since the by-product of the chemical decomposition of compost is heat, building a pile in the corner of a greenhouse creates a perfect free source of heat. Piles need to be turned regularly to generate adequate heat consistently.

SANDHILL ORGANICS AND PRAIRIE CROSSING
GRAYSLAKE, ILLINOIS

From the beginning, Vicky and George Ranney Jr. believed in having a farm. So, in 1987, when they bought 677 acres of prairie farmland north of Chicago for a mixed-use development, they dedicated 100 acres to growing food. "This land was always farmland," says Vicky, "so we considered what people would like to live next to. We realized that sooner or later there'd be a conflict between big agriculture and residential developments. People wouldn't find it comfortable to live next to pesticides and other chemicals."

Their investment paid off. The development, known as Prairie Crossing, sold all of its homes (about four hundred), and at a rate 34 percent above the market for similarly sized homes in the area. The one hundred acres of farmland is thriving, too. Sandhill Organics, run by husband-and-wife team Matt and Peg Sheaffer, operates on forty-five acres as a for-profit business farm. The majority of the remaining fifty-five acres is used by new, entrepreneurial farmers who are trying to start a business.

But the farmland is just one of many distinguishing factors of the project. A charter school, open land, trails, a swimming lake and beach, and a light-rail city connection contribute to the project's success in selling homes and creating a community. The large-scale intensive, integrated produce farm designed into the mixed-use residential development marks a huge leap for the peri-urban zone. The term *peri-urban* can be ambiguous, changing from city to city, but, generally, it refers to the land between the dense urban zone and the rural transect, often with a public transport connection such as light-rail, subway, or bus. Just a few years earlier, even the country's most progressive residential and mixed-use urban and peri-urban projects looked at small playscapes or raised-bed community garden plots as radical forms of green space.

Peg Sheaffer with some of her chickens. Planned communities like Prairie Crossing can offer cage-free chickens plenty of space to roam.

One hundred acres of organic production farmland distinguishes Prairie Crossing and connects it to the urban farm puzzle.

It takes almost an hour to drive from downtown Chicago north on I-94 to the town of Grayslake. The billboards, office "parks," and standard interstate commerce of gas stations and strip-mall retail dominate the corridor out of Chicago, but they eventually give way to the tall, mixed prairie grasses native to the Great Lakes plains. At the exit for Grayslake, the scene regains many of its original, rural characteristics.

The approach from the interstate to Grayslake and Prairie Crossing, however, travels down modern America's fuzzy middle ground between suburban and rural worlds. It's the classic peri-urban zone. A natural lake with tree snags and lily pads and marsh grasses covers a depression between a rim of trees and wild, hip-high grasses. A mile down the road, a fresh slab of pavement holds a large parking lot and a shopping center with chain stores. Beyond the pavement in Grayslake, more open land presents itself, along with expansive cornfields and a walled development of cookie-cutter homes with multiple pitched roofs, garages like the entrance to an Epcot cul-de-sac tunnel ride, and uniform yards of mowed green nonnative grasses.

The scene of retail, office park, and walled-off housing developments physically defines the food system we've developed in the last half century. It's a network of trucked and flown-in goods that consumers use their cars to gather and transport home. The only marginally "local"—and twenty-first-century—piece of the equation is the ethanol in the gasoline. But it has become widely apparent how the corn ethanol industry is ruining the farmland and the American family farms that can be seen from the Grayslake gas station. This land between city and farm is the battleground. Prairie Crossing's combination of residential and farm in the prairie marks a unique strategy in the shifting sands of agriculture and food systems.

A discussion of urban farms is compelled to migrate into the peri-urban world of low-density, single-family homes spread across vast acres of undeveloped land adjacent to a city. The most pressing question for the urban farm movement is how it will evolve. A common hope among urban farmers, from Fairview Gardens in California (page 39) to Jones Valley Urban Farm in Alabama (page 91) to Annie Novak and her rooftop patch in Brooklyn (page 117), is that their projects will reach a broad audience and propel an awareness of the importance of fresh, healthy local food. To truly transform our food system and create an industry of healthy food via a spectrum of micro- to macroproducers, as Katherine Kelly of Cultivate Kansas City (page 67)

insists we must do, we need the farmland that lies just outside our cities. That's where the acreage exists to produce the volume of sustainably grown food required to feed us. Many Americans live in peri-urban environments. It's easy to condemn the development of an automobile-dependent infrastructure of roads, services, and house farms that often replace the food farms, or to critique the definition of "success" to which many Americans subscribe: ownership of a single-family home with a double-vaulted ceiling, a two-car garage, a lawn to mow, and safety in community homogeny. But the peri-urban farm world, with its availability of land, is learning from the urban farms' ideas of high-yield planting patterns, social service benefits, and for-profit business opportunities.

Prairie Crossing has its place in the suburbanization of the rural world. It is a planned community of large homes that are affordable to only a certain economic stratum, and the development had to plow over many acres of prairie land to make it happen. But within the border of wild grasses that fringes the Prairie Crossing community (rather than the stucco wall that surrounds most planned developments), good ideas are shifting the paradigm of suburban and peri-urban development. With all the innovative farms and enterprising social-service programs sprouting in city

Matt and Peg Sheaffer in front of their silos. Instead of storing commodity crops, as they would on many of Illinois's large farms, these silos hold the tools and equipment used to produce the wide range of crops grown at Prairie Crossing.

Because the zoning at Sandhill Organics allows for agricultural uses, there are no regulations to prohibit chickens from roaming freely. The greater Grayslake community has been zoned as residential, so restrictions apply.

Sandhill Organics grows row crops on seventeen acres, yielding enough marketable produce to make the farm profitable.

farms throughout America, like the urban farms throughout this book, the success of Sandhill Organics farm marks a shining example of a potentially major resource for achieving food security.

Prairie Crossing was developed as a conservation community. Vicky and George Ranney Jr. set aside 60 percent of the 677 acres in a land-conservation easement, and an additional 3,200 acres are protected within the Liberty Prairie Reserve, a conglomeration of public and private land connected to the community.

The development is one of the earliest examples of what architect and planner Andrés Duany and others call agricultural urbanism. Duany and his colleagues have created a movement in the planning, developing, and architectural world with their New Urbanism model for sustainable design on a big-picture level that connects dense urban centers to farmland and wilderness via a series of progressively less dense "transects." New Urbanism wants to create a new language for coding, zoning, and design practices so that the builders of communities, cities, and even regions can employ the smart ideas of traditional communities that were less about the automobile and more about living smaller, more densely, more neighborly, closer to food sources, and, subsequently, incurring less societal and environmental impact.

Duany differentiates *agricultural urbanism* from *urban agriculture* in simple terms: agricultural urbanism creates the walkable urban form surrounded by agriculture, whereas urban agriculture is growing food on vacant lots and in backyards. He cites Detroit as a hub of urban agriculture, and he would call Prairie Crossing an example of agricultural urbanism, like Hampstead, in Montgomery, Alabama, and Mt Laurel, outside of Birmingham, Alabama.

Matt and Peg Sheaffer grow most of the food at Prairie Crossing. They came into the community early, as the original farmers for Sandhill Organics. They had been farming in Wisconsin, but when the Ranneys offered to lease them forty-five acres of certified organic farmland, they accepted. The Sheaffers moved into the farmhouse and they've made the operation a thriving business, thanks to CSA membership and sales at Chicago farmer's markets. They make a lot more money per acre (roughly $20,000 per acre) than the monocrop farmers (roughly $800 per acre) who dominate rural Illinois.

As noted earlier, Prairie Crossing has an additional fifty-five acres of farmland. The Learning Farm project uses some of the certified organic soil for youth programs that serve both elementary-school students and a diverse corps of high-school students from all over the county who work under the guidance of staff and college interns.

In the property's Back Forty, young farmers operate four "incubator farms" on which they grow produce and raise pigs and chickens. Participants in the Farm Business Development Center, these novices get the chance to create a viable, profitable farm business. When they're ready, they leave to create their own independent farms. It's a farm that grows farms and farmers.

So how does this work? And why doesn't it happen more often? Mike Sands is the executive director of the Liberty Prairie Foundation, a small private operating foundation within the Prairie Crossing community that supports land and resource conservation, civic management, food production (including the farms), and health-related education. Prior to coming to Prairie Crossing, Mike was the managing director of the Rodale Institute, a sixty-three-year-old organization that focuses on organic agriculture, both research and education. Sands has insight into the urban agriculture world that echoes the thoughts of Katherine Kelly in Kansas City, Annie Novak in Brooklyn, and other urban farmers who advocate a broad approach to food productivity and who recognize their own urban farms as a means to educate the larger, less urban population.

"The way to feed a city is through this peri-urban model," Mike says. "We're forty miles from the city loop, so we're there but we can deal in acres, not square footage.

"True urban farms are incredibly important, but if you consider food-productivity potential, it's limited. I do think we're ready for that next generation of urban farming: using waste heat to power year-round production. The urban farm can provide supplemental production, but its real value is as an entry point to food quality and why that matters. And it improves its immediate community, aesthetically and psychologically.

"The challenge with what we're doing here at Sandhill—not only diverse, integrated growing, but the marketing and financial planning involved—is that we don't have those farmers. If you offered twenty-thousand dollars an acre to an average farmer, he'd likely say he couldn't handle that. These [the Sheaffers and the incubator farmers] are entrepreneurs who pick farming as their business, not people who say they want to be farmers."

Mike sees successful farmers coming from four groups: liberal arts graduates, people going through a career change, recent immigrants, and the conventional farmer who has failed because of economic or personal constraints.

And so maybe this is the best place to end. A recurring question throughout an exploration of American urban farms in 2010 has been, which came first, the city or the farm? It is perhaps a rhetorical question, more like a riddle with a few answers. Prairie Crossing sits in the middle of the two, a mile from modern-American farmland and all its flaws and a half-hour train ride from one of the country's biggest cities. The land is here, but the knowledge and fervor for the new age of farming seem to be creeping out of the city, looking for more acres and new ways to make an independent living off the land. Fortunately, it looks and sounds like the good ole American way.

ESTABLISHED: 1994.

SIZE: The Prairie Crossing community comprises 677 acres, with 100 acres of certified organic farmland and 25 acres of pasture. Sandhill Organics leases 45 acres of the farmland.

MISSION: Liberty Prairie Foundation works to promote the integration of healthy ecosystems and the vibrant human communities throughout Lake County, Illinois. The foundation is particularly interested in projects that result in people acting in substantive ways to improve the environment and their communities. The Farm Business Development Center at Prairie Crossing supports the development of successful family farms by focusing on the production and marketing of organic foods for local and regional food systems.

WHO'S IN CHARGE: The nonprofit Liberty Prairie Foundation. Matt and Peg Sheaffer own and operate Sandhill Organics and employ a staff of six.

SURROUNDING NEIGHBORHOOD: Prairie Crossing community has 398 homes. The village of Grayslake has 23,000 people.

ZONING: Planned unit development with an underlying residential use.

FUNDING: Land cost was amortized over all of the 398 residences in the Prairie Crossing community and incorporated into the price paid by home purchasers. Liberty Prairie Foundation is funded by transaction fees, grants, and contracts. Sandhill Organics is a private, for-profit family farm dependent on the sale of its produce.

WHO EATS IT: Food is purchased at farmer's markets, through CSAs, and at farm stands. Every Friday the fields are gleaned for a local food pantry.

HOW TO Start an Urban Farm

Tucked behind a short prairie hill, beyond the windmill that provides some power to Sandhill Organics farm (and disguises a cell tower), hides the Back Forty of Prairie Crossing. It's actually fifty-five acres of certified organic soil where fruits, vegetables, and flowers aren't the only crops. The acreage holds a new generation of farmer entrepreneurs who are also setting roots in the rich soil.

The Liberty Prairie Foundation offers cheap leases of the development's land to newcomers who want to start their own farm businesses. It's a great scenario: available, fertile land, a sense of a safety net from the foundation, and the expertise of the Sheaffers at Sandhill Organics a few hundred yards away. The farmers can test their growing and, more important, their marketing and business skills before moving onto their own land. It's a wonderful progression of urban farm motivations and intensive farming skills into the larger-scale peri-urban and rural settings. But starting an urban or peri-urban farm business is daunting.

A similar program is unfolding at the Kansas City Center for Urban Agriculture, where the staff matches available land in the city with immigrants interested in starting a small farm-based business. After a two-year apprenticeship and participation in a matched-savings program, the new farmers are ready to scale their operation up and make a living.

Planning

Follow a few basic steps to make getting started go smoothly.

MISSION STATEMENT. Answer this question: What do you want to see changed as a result of your actions? This will become your mission statement.

RESOURCES. Now work backward. What resources do you have to make this change? Do you have access to land, to money, to people power?

OBJECTIVES. List the activities you want to do with the resources you have to achieve your desired change.

OUTCOMES. How will you know if you've been successful? Come up with a list of measurable goals that could result from your actions.

ACTION. Now, go make it happen!

Finding Land

Securing land is usually the first challenge when starting an urban farm project, though a growing number of residential and mixed-use developments, such as Prairie Crossing, are making this process easier than ever. But even if a development isn't offering land to potential urban farms, good options still exist. For example, Detroit literally has too much land to manage efficiently, so it is seeking ways to put farmers on previously occupied property. And Detroit is not the only city looking for urban farmers.

The founders of Jones Valley Urban Farm (JVUF) have started asking people in Birmingham if there is any available land for farming. The responses are often incredulous: "What do you mean you want to farm in the city?" "Why would you want to farm in the city?" But it takes only one person to understand. One day the JVUF founders were meeting with an accountant who was helping them apply for nonprofit status. After listening to what they wanted to do, the accountant looked out the window of his office and said, "What about that property?" He owned a few pieces of property across the street from his office that he had purchased years before as a long-term investment. The investment was still a long way from paying off, and he'd been stuck mowing the grass for years. The idea of someone else taking care of the property while he waited for an improved real-estate market seemed perfect. Jones Valley Urban Farm began that day. The cofounders walked out of the office, crossed the alley to the property, saw that there was some "workable" soil and sunlight, and said, "Let's start."

Where to Look for Urban Farmland

GOVERNMENT. It costs a lot of money to maintain unused land. Most municipalities will be eager to negotiate the idea of "less grass to mow." The city of Baltimore is soliciting urban farm business plans from the general public. It will lease city-owned land for free to anyone with a viable plan.

PRIVATE COMPANIES. Some cities are passing new taxation on storm-water drainage. A rooftop garden can actually save a company that has a large rooftop some money! If less water pours off the roof of a warehouse as a result of vegetation on the roof, the tax on that storm water will be less. So paying someone to farm the roof would actually be economically beneficial.

CHURCHES. Most congregations have a grass lawn that costs money to maintain. Check to see if there's interest in turning that lawn into a garden to feed the congregation—or the world.

SCHOOLS. Nearly every school in the country has some extra space for a garden. Try to partner with a school to provide space for students to grow food during the school year and for the community to grow food during the summer.

Picking the Right Spot

PROPERTY OWNERSHIP. Many urban gardeners squat on vacant land, but there's a serious risk of losing the land if property values increase and the owner (or city) suddenly wants to sell. Can you get a written lease for use of the property? You'd be surprised who will ask for back rent if they see you've been successful after using what was originally "donated" land.

SITE SECURITY. Fences can make a site seem secure, but a supportive community is a much better solution. Jones Valley Urban Farm provides neighbors with a portion of the farm to grow their own food. The neighbors get access to great affordable food, and JVUF gets a community looking after its property.

CLEAN SOIL. A land-use history can help you decide if you need further testing (see page 116).

SUNLIGHT. Most edible plants need a minimum of six hours of direct light to grow. Pruning trees can help, but consider finding a different location if trees need to be removed. It's expensive and there are *never* enough urban trees.

ACCESS TO WATER. Consistent access to water for irrigating plants is nonnegotiable for an urban farm. The harder it is to get water to the plants, the less likely it is the plants will get the water they need. Many cities will give urban farmers a discounted rate on water if they are not hooked up to the sewer. Los Angeles has created an urban agriculture water rate to give producers a discounted price on irrigation water. Wells in cities are often polluted or illegal. Rain catchment systems can be effective but need to be large enough to work well. For example, a three-hundred-gallon tank will run dry in an hour of regular watering.

Becoming Profitable

Financially successful farms all have one thing in common: they have matched a potential market for their products with the right scale of farming so that products are produced for less than they are sold for. Urban farmers face a unique challenge with this formula because the land available to farm is almost always small. To make a small operation profitable, urban farms have to take advantage of their unique characteristics to do the following two things.

Reduce Production Costs

- Access free land by extolling the benefits of converting unused land into something productive, beautiful, and healthy.

- Sell to local markets to reduce transportation costs. Or, even better, encourage customers to come to the farm for on-site sales.

- Utilize vegetable scraps from local restaurants to make compost for free.

- Develop relationships with local volunteer groups or alternative-sentencing programs to access free labor.

Increase Revenue

- Identify niche crops that are in high demand and need to be delivered frequently, such as microgreens. This almost always guarantees a high price.

- Develop a "brand name" that increases the value of products by tying the nontangible benefits of the farm to the name of the farm.

- Process produce into after-market products, such as salsa or pesto, to increase its value. Check with local health department codes to ensure compliance.

CONCLUSION
EDWIN MARTY

There are 20,000 acres of open land in Birmingham, 70,000 acres of open land in Philadelphia, and 100,000 vacant lots in Detroit. Yet farmland is being lost to urbanization at a staggering rate. Some 8 million acres of prime farmland has been covered with concrete in the last twenty years.

Today in America, we are three generations removed from the land. Most children growing up in cities have grandparents who had no connection to agriculture. Our lineage to an agriculturally based society has been completely severed. The knowledge accumulated over countless generations of how to produce food and how to protect the natural resources that enable us to live off the land is being lost. Farming, as an occupation, doesn't even appear on the most common census forms.

There's a need for a major agricultural shift in our nation. Ironically, the first stages of that change are happening in our cities, where the potential (vacant land) and the expertise (passionate, good-intentioned entrepreneurs) have become a sort of laboratory for ideas for new food systems. The next steps in this transformation will have to respond to the broader political, social, and economic changes occurring in our country.

Shifting Cities

America is facing tremendous changes as the twenty-first century unfolds, from the demographic makeup of the population to the resources available to perpetuate our lifestyles. All of these changes will have an impact on urban farming and whether or not it can continue to have a positive effect on our food system and the health of our populations and our environment. But what exactly are these changes, and are they permanent shifts or temporary fluctuations?

Americans are beginnning to understand that they have the potential to control where their food comes from and how they get it. The impacts will ripple widely.

It's now a fact that more people live in cities than in rural areas, both in America and throughout the world. Urban areas occupy only 2 percent of the land in the United States yet consume 75 percent of the energy. Unless something dramatic occurs, the trend toward greater density and energy consumption can be expected to continue.

While there is a steady trend toward urbanization in the United States, this shift is happening much faster in the developing world. Increasing urbanity inevitably leads to a greater demand for energy, consequently increasing energy costs. The United States is already feeling this pressure. As oil prices rise, our food system, which has relied on cheap fuel for the distribution of products, will not be able to continue without passing the increased costs on to the consumer. Americans will have to face the fact that spending less than 10 percent of household income on food will not be possible.

Urban areas in the United States will continue to reflect the overall trend toward an aging population, at least for the first half of the twenty-first century. Immigration could have an effect on that, depending on what policies (if any) are implemented. Gentrification of urban areas will shuffle certain demographics around cities, but probably won't affect their overall makeup.

An aging urban population is likely to increase the growing discrepancy in wealth, putting greater burdens on a shrinking workforce to provide for an expanding retirement population. Poverty rates will rise, causing increases in crime and the worsening of health indicators. Without significant intervention, urban obesity rates will continue to climb, directly impacting rates of diabetes and other diet-related diseases. Research clearly shows two trends being responsible for these increasing disease rates: poor dietary choices and limited opportunities for physical activity. Both of these issues are preventable with better planning and community engagement.

While these basic assumptions about the future of American cities are decidedly bleak, there are some potentially positive trends on the horizon, too. The demand for local, sustainably produced food may increase with the aging urban population. An interest in purchasing locally produced products directly from farmers, at farmer's markets, through CSAs, and at farm-to-plate restaurants has exploded in urban areas in the last decade and shows no sign of decreasing. Simultaneously, this same population is likely to demand increased green space, reduced sprawl, and better use of existing urban space generally.

Cities are also beginning to recognize and respond to gaps in low-income communities' access to fresh, local foods. "Food desert" studies across the country have clearly linked the prevalence of fast food to poor-health indicators. Farmer's markets, which have often only served outlying, wealthier consumers, are popping up in inner cities and quickly becoming a community's best outlet for healthy produce. Many of these markets are beginning to use electronic card-swipe machines to serve recipients of food stamps and of Women, Infants, and Children (WIC) food packages, often coupled with incentives like dollar-for-dollar matching for farmer's market purchases. This marks a major step toward food justice and urban farmers' capacity to reach a broad spectrum of their communities.

Urban Farm Response

These demographic trends and shifts are coupled with three distinct changes already under way in the urban farming movement. The first is a move toward for-profit urban farming. The last century of urban farming in America has focused almost exclusively on philanthropic urban farm projects that have "soft" outcomes, such as community development, job training, or food security. Only recently has the move toward farming in the city had a business focus, but this will undoubtedly increase as the following shifts unfold:

- The cost of food will increase due to rising fuel costs. Local food will soon become an economic necessity.
- Governments will recognize that a highly centralized food system is much more vulnerable to attack than a diversified food system. Urban farming will become part of a broader homeland security initiative.
- The industrialized food system will become increasingly less capable of providing the public with safe food. Consumers will value knowing their local farmers more than in the past.
- Urban planners will begin to include urban farms in urban in-fill and New Urbanist communities. Community development projects with an urban farm component, such as Prairie Crossing, will likely become far more common. Urban in-fill developments with food-growing components are also likely to become more widespread.

The second trend in American urban farming will be a growing acknowledgment of the urban farm's effectiveness at addressing real food security and food justice issues. The realities of these continuing successes will dictate which projects get the bulk of future funding and, therefore, what will prosper. The best programs will then become models for future urban farm entrepreneurs.

Strategies that actually make an impact in decreasing hunger and obesity will prosper, while strategies that simply "look" good won't. This may initially create tensions in the urban farm community, but will ultimately improve the efficiency of investments made in urban areas. While organizations such as the Community Food Security Coalition are working hard to provide urban farm projects with tools to evaluate their successes and plan for long-term sustainability, these efforts must be expanded to provide a much greater network of support. Evaluation will focus on the following criteria:

- What programs or components are most effective for an urban farm project to address local health outcomes?
- What are the best methods for evaluating and demonstrating the long-term impacts of these changes?
- What are the best means to "quantify" the nontangible benefits of urban farming, such as community engagement and beautification?
- Which urban farms provide the most replicable models for impacting a community's health while ensuring the project's long-term economic viability?

The third major trend will see urban farms as lightning rods that attract awareness and promote the taste for good, healthy food. This awareness is a natural consequence of a community's stronger connection to its food sources. Perhaps the biggest obstacle to growing awareness, however, is agriculture's lack of appeal to the next generation.

As the average age of the American farmer continues to rise, who will grow our food in the future? Can agriculture begin to attract the best and brightest of the next generation to contribute to vital discussions of food system issues? When was the last time a child said he or she wanted to grow up to be a farmer?

The declining interest in agriculture is probably due primarily to urban children not knowing any farmers or not seeing images of farming in popular culture apart from stereotypes. Food production has been moved to a factory or a warehouse, and forgotten. We've been told that our food is plentiful and cheap and that we should not worry about it and get back to more important things, such as solving unemployment or health problems—health problems that are often directly related to our poor diets or the unintended negative impacts of agriculture on our environment.

Urban farms have the potential to change the way youth perceive agriculture and its potential. As more urban farms sprout up around the country, driven by bright and capable entrepreneurs, children will see that farming can be a viable career and not just a last option. The appeal of urban farming is very different from that of traditional agriculture. Urban farmers don't have to make the same sacrifices as a farmer living in the country. All of the appealing social aspects of urban life that draw youth to the city are available to an urban farmer. The stereotype of toiling in the hot sun day in and day out while living in isolation is reversed for farmers growing viable crops in their backyards or on vacant lots down the street. Many of these farmers have part-time jobs in other industries, such as technology, and choose to spend part of their time working with their hands and cultivating something beautiful and healthy.

The message, then, being communicated to youth in inner-city, low-income communities with urban farms is especially potent. The idea that you can transform the negative aspects of your community by simply planting seeds is empowering. Since urban farms don't require much start-up capital, this vision is an approachable one for many communities.

Unlike a more traditional business such as a restaurant or grocery store that requires convincing someone to loan you money, an urban farm can be started with no more than recognition of a potential market for produce and acquisition of the technical skills to grow a product. Urban farmers, such as Mary Corboy in Philadelphia and Harry Rhodes in Chicago, are working hard to provide concrete examples of successful urban farms. Others are actively training low-income minority communities to take control over their food systems and grasp the power to decide for themselves what is available and affordable.

The Future of Urban Farms

Access to Capital

For urban farms' influence to continue to expand, such projects must be seen as economically viable. When urban youth see that urban farming can make money, a profound shift in participation will occur. For this to happen, the farms themselves must be scaled up to become profitable. Unfortunately, urban farms have a difficult time accessing capital for a number of reasons. Most traditional rural farms simply leverage their land for operational capital to expand. Few urban farmers own their own land and therefore can't use it as collateral.

Examples from *Breaking Through Concrete* point to some successful models for addressing this challenge, such as the small-farm-business training program at the Kansas City Center for Urban Agriculture and New Roots for Refugees Farm. At Prairie Crossing, a fee added to the purchase price of a new home helped the development's Sandhill Organics farm access start-up capital and move faster toward profitability—a clear benefit to the homeowners in their community.

Another option is for a community to develop a venture capital fund that prospective urban farmers can access when starting or scaling up. Local investors would receive a percentage of future earnings while giving the urban farmer the capacity to become profitable without the ownership of the farm, or the profits leaving the community.

Access to Technical Knowledge

While access to capital is critical to the success of any business, the knowledge of what to do with the investment is what determines long-term success. There is currently a significant void in the area of technical knowledge about sustainable agriculture and urban farming in urban areas across the country. Projects profiled in *Breaking Through Concrete,* such as the Homeless Garden Project in Santa Cruz and Growing Home in Chicago, are good beginnings. However, vocational training in secondary education and two-year college and community college programs must be developed for any appreciable impact to occur. Also, county extension offices must be encouraged to play a bigger role in the growth of urban farming. But this will only happen when the land-grant institutes that support county extension recognize urban farming as a "legitimate" enterprise worthy of their resources.

The other side of having technical knowledge is having access to the materials to implement that knowledge. There's simply no supply chain currently in place to get materials for urban farming. While box stores are often close by, urban farms need access to bulk supplies that these stores don't stock. This is another excellent business opportunity that has yet to be recognized in most American cities.

Access to Successful Business Models

Money and technical farming knowledge are the first two critical parts to expanding urban farming. The right business model, however, is what will make these projects successful over time. Understanding the correlation between a potential market for farm products and the right business structure to exploit that market can be challenging, especially for anyone without a formal business background. Growing up with parents who are successful business owners is usually the single best way to ensure future success. Unfortunately, such experience is rare in an inner city. Again, this is where vocational training could be developed to complement a technical training curriculum.

It's important to attract bright young minds to the urban farming movement and let them develop novel systems for responding to the potential market. Projects profiled in *Breaking Through Concrete*, like Eagle Street Rooftop Farm in Brooklyn and Greensgrow in Philadelphia, are giving urban farming an entirely different look and will undoubtedly attract new energy.

Policy That Supports Urban Farming

Today, the United States is experiencing an undeniable surge in urban farm activity. However, for this surge to have any long-term continuity, government policy must begin to shift quickly to support these efforts. There must be a recognition that current government policy adversely impacts the "real cost" of food and, therefore, the capacity for small farmers (urban farmers) to make a living. Can we shift what gets prioritized so that urban farms are subsidized as much as cotton and corn farms? A government that proactively supports a healthy food system will inevitably support urban farming.

Cities such as Seattle are paving the way by passing sweeping changes to local policy that open doors to new urban farm possibilities. These changes need to be translated so that other municipalities can easily adopt them and create similar opportunities. It's critical, however, to recognize that federal policy will never be able to do what local policy can. America is a diverse country with radically different forms of local government. The most powerful changes will occur when each municipality adopts good food policy based on local circumstances.

Land-Use Planning

The majority of urban farms in America are growing on less than one acre. This makes the basic economics of an operation difficult over time. With an increase in access to land that comes with a broader understanding of urban farming's advantages, projects should be able to expand to match potential markets with production capacity.

Traditional agricultural models look at matching abundant affordable land with available labor and then transporting products to the market. Urban agriculture turns this model around and matches abundant undervalued urban land with abundant urban labor and then brings the market to the farm. Rust Belt cities, such as Detroit, Pittsburgh, and Birmingham, all have tremendous amounts of vacant land that could be made available to urban farming with the right zoning and planning. Mike Scroll, president of Hantz Farms in Detroit, is looking at hundreds of acres of vacant urban land for large-scale agricultural production, and even tree farms. While some in Detroit don't share his vision of a big corporate urban farm, he does point to a scale that actually could make a difference in both the economics of a city and the broader food system.

For the next generation of American cities to prosper, planners have to rethink the place of agriculture in a hierarchy of uses. "The definition of 'best use' puts agriculture at the bottom of the heap," says Smith, speaking about Detroit. "There's this hope that manufacturing will somehow rise again as an engine of economic support, that all of the jobs will come back and all of the people will come back. As much as light industry and manufacturing did to build this town, we can't rely on it anymore." Urban farms just might be these cities' best hope.

Development of New Markets

Urban farming's greatest potential may lie in its ability to create interest in locally produced food. Connecting consumers with their food generates knowledge about the potential impacts of their choices. When more people vote with their fork, there will be a bigger and growing market for good food. Urban farms are not unlikely to be able to meet the demands of this market. Rural farms will benefit directly from the expansion of urban farms, as more and more customers show up at farmer's markets and look for CSAs. Urban farms will also increasingly interact with large urban institutions, such as schools, hospitals, and churches. These markets will engender new connections with farms surrounding urban areas and create a much stronger food system.

Numerous examples in *Breaking Through Concrete* illustrate how an urban farm can help develop a market that's greater than the urban farm's capacity to meet it. Greensgrow, Fairview Gardens, and Jones Valley Urban Farm have all developed relationships with rural farmers who supplement the urban farms' CSAs. This model is likely to become much more popular, especially as nonprofit urban farms recognize the potential to cover the cost of education and outreach programs through additional sales revenue.

Diggin' In

The urban farm movement will be built on a dense existing foundation. But it's clear the world we live in today will not be the same one we live in tomorrow. Can urban farms embrace these changes without a catastrophe that forces urban areas to alter their course?

Urban farming so far has been about demonstration. The next step will be to scale up the projects. There are some notable examples of cities, such as Havana, Cuba, producing significant amounts of an urban population's caloric needs. In the early 1990s, Havana was forced to reorient its entire structure after the collapse of the Soviet Union left the country without access to cheap imported food and synthetic chemicals to produce its own. The Cubans responded to this catastrophe by breaking through concrete and planting every available piece of land in the city. Entire industries were created overnight to supply locally produced compost to urban farmers, and the country averted mass starvation. While food was not abundant, there was at least enough to feed the people. Could America respond in a similar way without a disaster forcing it?

Even with a tremendous increase in the number (and efficiency) of urban farms, our urban areas will likely still be heavily dependent on traditional agriculture for the bulk of their sustenance into the foreseeable future. So the real, short- to medium-term potential of urban farming lies in its capacity to educate future generations of advocates of a healthy food system.

Our country is in serious need of a shift in how we think about and relate to our food. We have been taught for generations, and come to expect, that because of our highly efficient modern agricultural techniques, food should be cheap. We've also been taught that because of advances in food-safety science, our food is completely safe. Both of these assumptions stem from our trust in a centralized regulatory system that, presumably, is always looking out for our best interests. With sharp increases in diet-related disease and food-safety issues, the current assumptions about our centralized food system are increasingly being called into question.

We, as citizens, as Americans, can take personal responsibility for how our food is produced, processed, and consumed. It is no longer acceptable to assume that someone else, somewhere out there, has our best interests in mind, and that they have the ability to assure us of our food's safety. We can become "reacquainted" with our food. Good, healthy food will not simply appear in our communities without our demanding it and actively creating connections between producers and consumers. Fortunately, urban farming is the perfect vehicle for connecting those dots. Urban farms across the country will serve to train the next generation of farmers in sustainable food-production techniques, educate the next generation of consumers about why good, healthy food is critical for our survival, and inspire individuals to seek these changes in their own communities.

Imagine a community built around urban farms producing safe, healthy food. Imagine that these urban farms are just one part of a resilient web of food producers tied together through a wide variety of markets owned by the people who live in that community. Imagine growing up in such a community, knowing that the land surrounding your home is where your sustenance comes from and, if you choose, where your livelihood comes from. Imagine the children growing up in these communities eating fresh, locally produced food and understanding the power that flows from the soil, through their bodies, and into every part of their lives. This is a world we can create. It's waiting just underneath the concrete . . .

An old chair at Detroit's D-Town Farm sits next to a row of vegetables. Edible mushrooms will eventually emerge from the cushions.

ACKNOWLEDGMENTS

We did not just sit down in a library and write this book. We had to get out and see the farms. The cross-country tour would not have happened without the support of Why-Hunger, a leading nonprofit advocate for innovative, community-based solutions to hunger and poverty. WhyHunger's Brooke Smith was a constant presence throughout the project, providing vital resources and insights.

We would also like to thank good friend and videographer-filmmaker Charlie Hoxie, who took his summer break from graduate school in documentary film to sweat through two months with us on the short bus and in the minivan. Charlie recorded dozens of hours of videotape, from poignant farmer interviews to roadside bus break-downs. His work appears on the book's Web site and offers a vivid illustration of the people and places behind the book.

To our families and friends who supported us along the way. To the staff and board of directors at Jones Valley Urban Farm for helping to create an amazing organization that laid the foundation for much of this book. To Andrea and Edie Marty, who can now have back their father and husband, respectively.

And, of course, to all the farmers who have created these projects and who let us document them for a few days. Their passion, intention, and authenticity were inspirational throughout the process.

RECOMMENDED READING

Ableman, Michael. *On Good Land: The Autobiography of an Urban Farm*. San Francisco: Chronicle Books, 1998.

Carpenter, Novella. *Farm City: The Education of an Urban Farmer*. New York: Penguin Press, 2009.

Flores, H.C. *Food Not Lawns: How to Turn Your Yard into a Garden and Your Neighborhood into a Community*. White River Junction, VT: Chelsea Green, 2006.

Girardet, Herbert. *Creating Sustainable Cities*. Devon, UK: Green Books, 1999.

Hynes, H. Patricia. *A Patch of Eden: America's Inner City Gardens*. White River Junction, VT: Chelsea Green, 1996.

Kellogg, Scott, and Stacy Pettigrew. *Toolbox for Sustainable City Living*. Cambridge, MA: South End Press, 2008.

Koc, Mustafa, Rod MacRae, Jennifer Welsh, and Luc Mougeot, eds. *For Hunger-Proof Cities: Sustainable Urban Food Systems*. Ottawa, Canada: International Development Research Center, 1999.

Kunstler, James Howard. *The Geography of Nowhere: The Rise and Decline of America's Man-Made Landscape*. New York: Simon & Schuster, 1993.

Lawson, Laura J. *City Bountiful: A Century of Community Gardening in America*. Berkeley: University of California Press, 2005.

Mougeot, Luc, ed. *Agropolis: The Social, Political and Environmental Dimensions of Urban Agriculture*. London: Earthscan and International Development Research Center, 2005.

Nordahl, Darrin. *Public Produce: The New Urban Agriculture*. Washington, DC: Island Press, 2009.

Olson, Michael. *MetroFarm: The Guide to Growing for Big Profit on a Small Parcel of Land*. Santa Cruz, CA: TS Books, 1994.

Peacock, Paul. *The Urban Farmer's Handbook*. Preston, UK: Good Life Press, 2008.

Register, Richard. *Ecocities: Rebuilding Cities in Balance with Nature*. Vancouver: New Society Publishers, 2006.

Viljoen, Andre. *Continuous Productive Urban Landscapes: Designing Urban Agriculture for Sustainable Cities*. Burlington, MA: Architectural Press, 2005.

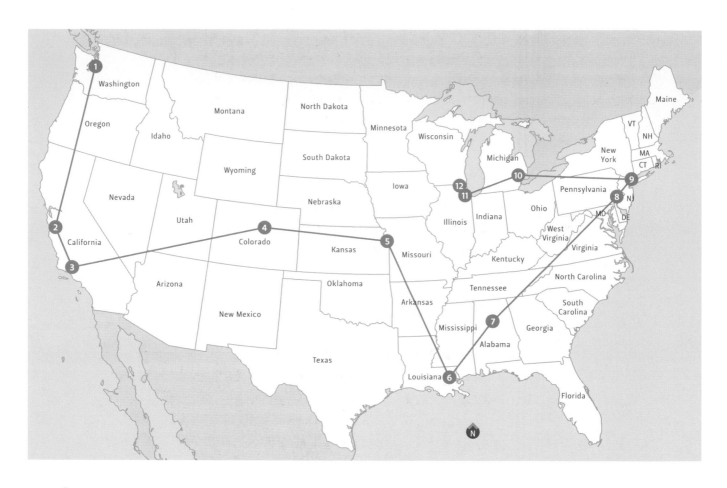

1 Seattle, Washington · P-Patch Community Garden Program

2 Santa Cruz, California · Homeless Garden Project

3 Santa Barbara, California · Fairview Gardens and the Center for Urban Agriculture

4 Denver, Colorado · Denver Urban Gardens

5 Kansas City, Kansas and Missouri · Juniper Gardens and Cultivate Kansas City

6 New Orleans, Louisiana · Versailles Community

7 Birmingham, Alabama · Jones Valley Urban Farm

8 Philadelphia, Pennsylvania · Greensgrow Farms and the Philadelphia Project

9 Brooklyn, New York · Eagle Street Rooftop Farm

10 Detroit, Michigan · Catherine Ferguson Academy

11 Chicago, Illinois · Wood Street Urban Farm and Growing Home

12 Grayslake, Illinois · Sandhill Organics and Prairie Crossing

DAVID HANSON is a freelance journalist living in Seattle. He was the founding travel editor of *Cottage Living* magazine and is now a contributing editor for *Coastal Living* and *Southern Living*. His writing has also appeared in *Garden and Gun*, *Preservation*, and *Sunset*.

MICHAEL HANSON shoots for the *New York Times, Outside, Patagonia, Coastal Living, Budget Travel*, and *Sunset*, among other publications. He was recently named one of the World's Top Travel Photographers by *Popular Photography* magazine.

EDWIN MARTY is the founder and former executive director of Jones Valley Urban Farm in downtown Birmingham, Alabama. Edwin began Jones Valley while he was a garden editor at *Southern Living* magazine. He is now the executive director for the Hampstead Institute in Montgomery, Alabama.

MARK WINNE is the author of *Food Rebels, Guerrilla Gardeners, and Smart-Cookin' Mamas: Fighting Back in an Age of Industrial Agriculture.*

University of California Press, one of the most distinguished university presses in the United States, enriches lives around the world by advancing scholarship in the humanities, social sciences, and natural sciences. Its activities are supported by the UC Press Foundation and by philanthropic contributions from individuals and institutions. For more information, visit www.ucpress.edu.

University of California Press
Berkeley and Los Angeles, California

University of California Press, Ltd.
London, England

© 2012 by The Regents of the University of California

Library of Congress Cataloging-in-Publication Data

Hanson, David, 1978–
    Breaking through concrete : building an urban farm revival / David Hanson and Edwin Marty ; photographs by Michael Hanson ; with a foreword by Mark Winne.
        p.   cm.
    Includes bibliographical references.
    ISBN 978-0-520-27054-1 (cloth : alk. paper)
    1. Urban agriculture—United States.   2. Community gardens—United States.
I. Marty, Edwin, 1972–   II. Hanson, Michael, 1981–   III. Title.
    S494.5.U72H36   2012
    630.9173'2—dc23

                                                                          2011024485

Designer and compositor: Lia Tjandra
Text: Leitura Sans
Display: Ultramagnetic
Prepress: Embassy Graphics
Printer and binder: CS Graphics, Pte. Ltd.

Printed in Singapore

21   20   19   18   17   16   15   14   13   12
10   9   8   7   6   5   4   3   2   1

The paper used in this publication meets the minimum requirements of ANSI/NISO Z39.48-1992 (R 1997) (*Permanence of Paper*).